It's All About
Science

4

Mukul Sahgal

This Book Belongs to :

Name ....

Roll No...

Class and Section ....

School ....

S. CHAND
School

S. CHAND SCHOOL BOOKS

(An imprint of S. Chand Publishing)
A Division of S. Chand And Company Limited
(An ISO 9001 : 2008 Company)
7361, Ram Nagar, Qutab Road, New Delhi-110055
Phone: 23672080-81-82, 9899107446, 9911310888; Fax: 91-11-23677446
www.schandpublishing.com; e-mail : helpdesk@schandpublishing.com

Branches :

Ahmedabad   : Ph: 27541965, 27542369, ahmedabad@schandpublishing.com
Bengaluru   : Ph: 22268048, 22354008, bangalore@schandpublishing.com
Bhopal   : Ph: 4274723, 4209587, bhopal@schandpublishing.com
Chandigarh   : Ph: 2625356, 2625546, 4025418, chandigarh@schandpublishing.com
Chennai   : Ph: 28410027, 28410058, chennai@schandpublishing.com
Coimbatore   : Ph: 2323620, 4217136, coimbatore@schandpublishing.com (Marketing Office)
Cuttack   : Ph: 2332580, 2332581, cuttack@schandpublishing.com
Dehradun   : Ph: 2711101, 2710861, dehradun@schandpublishing.com
Guwahati   : Ph: 2738811, 2735640, guwahati@schandpublishing.com
Hyderabad   : Ph: 27550194, 27550195, hyderabad@schandpublishing.com
Jaipur   : Ph: 2219175, 2219176, jaipur@schandpublishing.com
Jalandhar   : Ph: 2401630, 5000630, jalandhar@schandpublishing.com
Kochi   : Ph: 2809208, 2808207, cochin@schandpublishing.com
Kolkata   : Ph: 23353914, 23357458, kolkata@schandpublishing.com
Lucknow   : Ph: 4026791, 4065646, lucknow@schandpublishing.com
Mumbai   : Ph: 22690881, 22610885, mumbai@schandpublishing.com
Nagpur   : Ph: 6451311, 2720523, 2777666, nagpur@schandpublishing.com
Patna   : Ph: 2300489, 2302100, patna@schandpublishing.com
Pune   : Ph: 64017298, pune@schandpublishing.com
Raipur   : Ph: 2443142, raipur@schandpublishing.com (Marketing Office)
Ranchi   : Ph: 2361178, ranchi@schandpublishing.com
Sahibabad   : Ph: 2771235, 2771238, delhibr-sahibabad@schandpublishing.com

First Published in 2017
Second Impression 2018

ISBN : 978-93-525-3256-8   Code: SCS2AAS040SCIAA17ICN

PRINTED IN INDIA

By Vikas Publishing House Pvt. Ltd., Plot 20/4, Site-IV, Industrial Area Sahibabad, Ghaziabad-201010 and Published by S. Chand And Company Limited, 7361, Ram Nagar, New Delhi -110 055.

Preface

It's All About Science is a series of science books for primary school designed to meet the learning outcomes stated in the latest CISCE syllabus.

The primary objective of the series is to develop scientific attitude in children. To achieve this, it aims to arouse the curiosity of children to know more, and emphasize understanding of concepts, development of independent thinking and experimental skills, and ability to apply knowledge in everyday situations.

Key Features

Key concepts define the focus of the chapter, as laid down in the syllabus guidelines.

Each chapter begins with a **Warming up** activity to make the children think and participate, thus getting them into a receptive state of mind for absorbing new knowledge.

Development of skills such as application, thinking and experimental skills is given special importance.

The text is designed to **develop understanding** rather than simply providing information, using simple language and attractive illustrations.

Linked Internet Sites open up the world to the child through the Internet – children can learn more about whatever arouses their curiosity at their own pace.

Points to remember enables quick recap.

Variety of Exercises help to assess the effectiveness of the teaching programme in meeting the stated objectives.

- MCQs
- True and false
- Fill in the blanks
- Matching
- Crossword puzzles and Word grids
- Very short answer questions

Mind maps bring conceptual clarity.

Thinking questions develop higher order thinking skills.

Science in daily life enables children to understand the world around them and to develop application skill.

Projects emphasize learning by doing and develop experimental skills.

Two **Test papers** help in continuous assessment.

SYLLABUS
(CLASS IV)

Theme 1: Human Body: Food We Eat

The underlying aim of this theme is to provide information about and discuss the various components of food and also develop an awareness regarding the importance of eating a balanced nutritious diet. The content would further help in developing skills such as, i.e., classification, and sensitivity towards environment and sensitivity towards wastage of food.

Learning Outcomes:

Children will be able to:

- discuss and share various kind of food items used by a family on various occasions;
- list out food items based on 'energy giving', 'body building' and 'protection from diseases';
- classify food items into various components based on their function and cite examples of each component of food;
- explain the need for balanced diet in their own words;
- discuss the need of each food component for healthy living;
- infer why different groups of people require different amount and kinds of food (child, adult, elders, etc.);
- suggest various ways to avoid food wastage;
- appreciate the need and importance of plants/ environment in our life;
- develop a sensitivity towards plants and the environment.

Human Body: Food We Eat

Key Concepts/Concerns	Suggested Transactional Processes
Revisit concepts/ skills of learnt in Class III. • Food for energy, for work, food for growth (body building), food for protection from diseases. • Components of food: Carbohydrates, Proteins, Fats, Vitamins, Minerals, Water and roughage as essential components. • Examples of each group of food component. • An idea of a balanced diet. • Care of food to avoid wastage.	• Revisit concepts learnt in Class III and build on previous learning. • Providing opportunities to children to share their personal experiences about the food they generally eat, what they like and do not like, different kinds of food available around them etc.; • Providing opportunities to children to observe various kinds of food items, and list out those that provide energy, vitamins, minerals, body building/wear & tear (actual/ visuals); • Organizing group activities to classify food items based on their functions (energy giving, body building and protection from diseases); • Showing documentary films/charts on balanced diet and later organizing a discussion; • Conducting individual activities by asking each child to make a menu of one week keeping the need for a balanced diet in view (under supervision of elders). • Discussing / interacting with the Dietician. • Assigning individual/group projects to children on: • Drawing pictures/ collecting pictures of each kind of group of food; • Preparing a component-wise chart on different food items with examples. • Discussing ways to avoid food wastage. • Conducting activities in the school (tree plantation, care of plants) to develop a habit for care and protection of plants.

Suggested Learning Resources:

- Live experience of children related to food.
- Various kinds of food items (actual).
- Picture cards of different food items and their role.
- Documentary film on a balanced diet.
- Doctor and/or Dietician.
- Charts and visuals on food items.
- Magazines describing more information on food items (food of children, adults, elders).
- Children's portfolio
- Children's drawings.
- Worksheets provided/prepared by the teacher.

Integration: Languages, Health and Physical Education, Social Studies (Our State - Agriculture (Types of Crops))

Life Skills: Sensitivity towards plants/environment, appreciating the value of avoiding wastage of food.

Theme 2: Human Body: The Teeth

The main focus of this theme is to create awareness regarding the various kinds of teeth in human beings and the importance of dental care and regular check-ups. The theme will also focus on the need for daily brushing to keep teeth healthy and strong for healthy living.

Learning outcomes:

Children will be able to:

- identify and name the different kinds of teeth in human beings;
- draw pictures of each kind of tooth and label the parts of a tooth;
- discuss the need for various kinds of teeth in human beings and explain their functions;
- infer why the old people, adults and children have different number of teeth;
- demonstrate healthy habits related to taking care of their teeth;
- give reasons why the gums and teeth get spoilt/damaged;
- suggest ways to keep teeth and gums healthy and strong;
- appreciate the importance of regular check-up of teeth;
- relate healthy food habits with the development of healthy teeth and proper brushing.

Human Body: The Teeth

Key Concepts/Concerns	Suggested Transactional Processes
• Kind of teeth in the mouth and location. • Structure and Functions of each kind of tooth. • Diagram with labelling of parts of a tooth, number of teeth of each kind in: infants and adults. • Care of Teeth and Gums: Causes of cavities/deficiencies and steps to prevent them. • Need for regular check-up to keep teeth healthy; importance of healthy dental care habits. • Role of food in the development of healthy teeth and gums.	• Providing opportunities to children to share their personal experiences (when did milk teeth first appear, how many teeth do they have, etc.) • Organizing simple activities individually and in small groups with children such as: • Counting one's own teeth and sharing with the peer group; • Visiting a dentist/ inviting a dentist to conduct a question answer session in the class; Organizing discussion in small groups on care of teeth; • Providing opportunities to draw pictures of kinds of teeth and labelling them; • Making models of various types of teeth; • Showing a documentary on care of teeth/steps showing the process to clean teeth followed by group activities to demonstrate healthy ways of brushing one's teeth. • Maintaining children's portfolio to keep their medical report for regular check-ups. • Discussing / interacting with the Dentist.

Suggested Learning Resources:

- Children's own experiences.
- Tooth brush, Tongue cleaner
- Pictures on the process of cleaning the teeth, tongue etc.
- Film on care of teeth.
- Magnifying glass to observe teeth/gums.
- Medical reports of children.

Integration: Health and Physical Education

Life skills: Healthy habits for a healthy living

Theme 3: Human Body: The Digestive & Excretory Systems

The main objective of this theme is to create an awareness and understanding regarding the functioning of the digestive and the excretory systems in the human body. The theme also aims at to promoting healthy habits for healthy living. While transacting this theme, the concepts covered in this theme may be related with the themes 'Food we Eat' and 'The Teeth' to develop a better understanding on related concepts.

Learning Outcomes:

Children will be able to:

- draw and label parts of the digestive system;
- name and identify organs of the digestive system;
- discuss the functions of the digestive system in the human body;
- explain the functions of each digestive organ in his/her own words;
- give reasons for chewing of food for better digestion;

- name and identify organs of the excretory system;
- explain and functions of each organ of the excretory system;
- draw and label parts of the excretory system;
- discuss the need for the excretory system in the body;
- identify various habits that help to keep the digestive and excretory organs healthy.

Human Body: The Digestive and Excretory Systems

Key Concepts	Suggested Transactional Processes
• Organs of the digestive system (mouth, food pipe, stomach, liver, small and large intestine, rectum, anus). • Functions of various organs in digestion, need for chewing food well, and for regular bowel movements. • Need for water. • Organs of the excretory system and their functions. • Healthy habits related to digestion and excretion.	• Providing opportunities to children to share their own experiences. • Drawing attention to the various organs in a model/chart of the digestive and excretory systems. • Opportunities to draw pictures of both the systems and labelling the organs in both the systems. • Discussing the importance of water in the process of digestion and excretion. • Discussing the functions of the different organs of the digestive and excretory systems, through models/charts. • Discussing healthy food habits related to digestion and excretion and relating them with the children's own experiences

Suggested Learning Resources:
- Pictures/charts of the digestive and excretory systems.
- Models showing various organs of digestive and excretory systems.
- e-programme/content on digestive/excretory systems.
- Cut out of the human body locating places of various organs of both the systems.
- Diagrams on the digestive and excretory systems made by children.
- Discussion on junk and healthy food items

Integration: Languages, Health and Physical Education.

Theme 4: Adaptation in Animals

The theme 'Adaptation in animals' would discuss need for adaptation in animals by referring to the different habitats. The theme would also discuss adaptations seen in the bodies of herbivores, omnivores and carnivores. Some key concepts such as need for adaptation, reasons for adaptation in animals would also be discussed to create awareness amongst children by using various examples.

Learning Outcomes:
Children will be able to:
- discuss the need for adaptation in animals to survive in their different habitats;
- enlist reasons of adaptation in animals: on land, in air and in water;
- give examples of adaptations of animals: on land and in water;
- relate modification of body parts in various animals due to food habits (herbivores, carnivores, omnivores);
- give examples of herbivores, carnivores and omnivores;
- develop empathy, love and concern for animals.

Adaptation in Animals

Key Concepts/Concerns	Suggested Transactional Processes
• Adaptation in animals. • Need for adaptations in animals. • Reasons of adaptations. • Examples of adaptations in animals: on land, in water. • Adaption in modification of body parts in herbivores, carnivores, omnivores. • Examples of each. • Care and concern for animals	• Sharing/listening to the experiences of children related to adaptation in animals. • Showing a film/picture and then creating situations to identify adaptations in various animals have. • Assigning project work to children in groups/individually to develop charts depicting adaptation in animals due to water, land, food habits; • Assigning Project work to children in groups/individually to develop scrap books on adaptations in animals.

Suggested Learning Resources:
- Pictures of animals having adaptations.
- Flash cards.
- Digital images (in animals).
- Web map of animals showing adaptations on land.
- Web map of animals showing adaptations in water.
- Charts prepared by children.
- Documentary film on adaptation in animals.

Integration: Languages, Health and Physical Education, Social Studies (Our State-Landforms, Climate, vegetation)
Life Skills: Care and concern for animals

Theme 5: Adaptation in Plants

The theme 'Adaptations in Plants' is expected to provide awareness and information regarding the need for adaptation in plants on land, in water and due to variation in habitat, along with examples. The theme would also be expected to develop skills related to observation, concern and care for plants.

Learning Outcomes:
Children will be able to:
- discuss the need for adaptation in plants to survive in their habitat;
- enlist reasons of adaptations in plants on land, water, desert and hilly areas;
- give examples of plant adaptations on land, water, desert and hilly areas;
- draw pictures of various adaptations in plants.

Adaptation in Plants

Key Concepts/Concerns	Suggested Transactional Processes
<ul><li>Need for adaptation in plants.</li><li>Examples of adaptation of plants on land with examples.</li><li>Examples of adaptation of plants in water with examples.</li><li>Examples of adaptation of plants in desert with examples.</li><li>Examples of adaptation of plants in hilly areas with examples.</li></ul>	<ul><li>Sharing/listening to the learning experiences of children related to adaptation in plants.</li><li>Showing various plants having adaptations due to their habitats.</li><li>Creating situations to identify various other plants having (after seeing pictures/films) adaptations.</li><li>Assigning project work to:</li><li>develop charts depicting adaptation of plants in different habitats i.e. water, land,</li><li>develop scrap book on adaptation in different plants with examples</li><li>Drawing of pictures by children of different adaptations seen in plants.</li></ul>

Suggested Learning Resources:
- Pictures.
- Flash cards.
- Digital images (various plants).
- Web map of plants showing adaptations.
- Examples of adapted plants.
- Charts prepared by children.
- Documentary film on adaptation in plants.

Integration: Languages, Social Studies (Our State-Landforms, rivers, climate, vegetation)
Life skills: Concern for the environment

Theme 6: Plants in the Surroundings and Environment

The aim of this theme is to acquaint children with the classification of plants and functions of different parts of plants. The functions of leaves along with the processes of transpiration and photosynthesis will also be discussed in a simple manner. The theme would also highlight the significance of plants in our lives by taking different examples from children's daily lives.

Learning Outcomes:
Children will be able to:
- identify plants as herbs, shrubs and trees;
- identify the kind of roots seen in plants (through observation);
- differentiate between tap and fibrous root (through observation);
- cite examples of plants with the tap and fibrous root systems;
- draw pictures and label each kind of root system;
- identify variations in leaves (observation);
- discuss the process of photosynthesis in their own words (simple non-technical language);
- demonstrate presence of iodine in a leaf through a simple experiment (with support of elders).

Plants in the Surroundings and Environment

Key Concepts/Concerns	Suggested Transactional Processes
• Parts of plants and their uses (Revisiting earlier concepts). • Roots: kinds of roots, their functions and examples. • Shoots: functions of the stem. • Functions of the leaf: Photosynthesis, transpiration process (in simple language). • Iodine test for starch in leaves. • Products obtained from plants such as food items, wood, coir, rubber, fibres.	• Providing opportunities to observe various kinds of plants and categorizing them as herbs, shrubs and trees. • Drawing pictures of leaves and colouring them. • Showing through simple experiments different functions of the leaf (showing stomata, green pigment) to explain transpiration, photosynthesis (in simple language using non-scientific terms). • Conducting simple experiments/activities (hand lens) to locate stomata on the surface of leaf • Providing opportunities to children to discuss various uses of plant products in our life, with examples • Conducting experiment to demonstrate the process of photosynthesis • Conducting experiment showing presence of starch in leaves using iodine test • Providing opportunities to appreciate the significance of plants in our life. • Creating a herbal garden

Suggested Learning Resources
- Various kind of leaves, different parts of plants
- Plant products-wood, coir, rubber.
- Hand lens.
- Apparatus required for experiments on photosynthesis and presence of iodine in leaves.
- Visuals /videos on the use of plants.
- Collection of products of plants.
- School's herbal garden.

Life Skills: Sensitivity towards plants and environment.

Theme 7: Air

'Air' is an important component for our life. Many activities are carried out with the help of air. This theme will help to develop clarity in children regarding properties of air, besides discussing the causes of air pollution and remedies for the same. The theme is also expected to develop experimental and observational skills.

Learning Outcomes:
Children will be able to:
- give reasons why air is important for living beings;
- demonstrate some properties of air through simple experiments (air has weight, occupies space, expands and has no colour);
- demonstrate the process of inhalation/exhalation of air;
- discuss causes of air pollution in the environment / surroundings;
- suggest ways/remedies to reduce air pollution in the environment;
- show concern about the environmental activities which cause air pollution.

Air

Key Concepts/Concerns	Suggested Transactional Processes
• Some properties of air i.e., occupy space, weight, expands, no colour. • Composition of air (gases + water vapour). • Process of breathing and burning. • Causes of air pollution – dust, smoke, spitting (germs/bacteria, Virus), preventive measures to keep air clean.	• Revisiting concepts learnt in the earlier classes. • Building on children's earlier learning. • Conducting simple experiments to demonstrate that air has weight, occupies space, air expands. • Arranging live demonstration to show the process of inhalation/ exhalation of air by lungs. • Arranging a class activity for all children to demonstrate the process of breathing and deep breathing for healthy living. • Organizing group discussions to identify causes of air pollution. • Assigning projects (group work) to children to list down ways to prevent air pollution. • Facilitating origami activities with children like making kites, aeroplanes, etc. • Decorating the classroom by making small kites.

Suggested Learning Resources:
- Apparatus /objects required to conduct experiments.
- Project work report on causes of air pollution.
- Project work report on ways to prevent air pollution.
- Origami material.

Integration: Languages, Health and Physical Education, Social Studies (Pollution- its impact on the environment, The Earth- Atmosphere)

Theme 8: Materials and Solutions

The theme 'Materials and Solutions' is expected to develop in children an understanding of the meaning 'solute', 'solvent' and 'solution' through daily life examples. The theme would also deal with various methods of separation of insoluble material from water/liquids.

Learning Outcomes:

Children will be able to:

- discuss/share examples of solvent, solute and solution in day-to-day life;
- explain each term in their own words;
- conduct experiments to make solutions by using solute and solvent;
- identify various methods of separation of solute and solvent from solution;
- distinguish between the methods of sedimentation, filtration and evaporation;
- give an example of the methods of - sedimentation, filtration and evaporation;
- differentiate between soluble and insoluble substances in liquids;
- cite examples of soluble and insoluble substances.

Materials and Solutions

Key Concepts/Concerns	Suggested Transactional Processes
Revisit learning of Class III • Definition- solvent, solute and solution, giving examples of each (simple language). • Soluble and insoluble substances giving examples of each (solubility in oil, water) • Method of separation: sedimentation, decantation, filtration, evaporation.	• Building on previous learning and concepts. • Conducting simple experiments to demonstrate how to make solutions in various solvents. • Conducting activities/ to demonstrate various ways of separating impurities from a solution. • Conducting simple experiments showing soluble and insoluble substance in solvent. • Encouraging children to cite examples of various solutions used in day-to-day life. • Citing examples of the process of sedimentation, decantation, filtration and evaporation. • Demonstrating to children in groups and as a whole class: • the process of sedimentation (sand + water, clay + water); • the process of decantation, filtration and evaporation (sugar in water).

Suggested Learning Resources:
- Collection of soluble and insoluble substances.
- Apparatus to show making of a solution.
- Sieving apparatus, filter paper.
- Apparatus to show evaporation activity.

Theme 9: Light

The expectation of this theme is to create awareness about various sources of light in the environment and simple properties of light, by taking examples from daily life. The theme is also expected to provide an understanding of how a shadow is formed and various uses of natural sources of light. The theme would also focus on how to save and conserve light energy in our day-to-day lives.

Learning Outcomes:

Children will be able to:

- identify various sources and uses of light in the environment;
- distinguish between natural and artificial sources of light;
- cite examples of natural and artificial sources of light;
- appreciate the use of natural source of light in our day-to-day life;
- differentiate between luminous and non-luminous objects;
- differentiate between transparent, translucent and opaque objects in the surroundings;
- cite examples of each type of object, i.e. transparent, translucent and opaque;
- explain the process of shadow formation in simple language.

Light

Key Concepts/Concerns	Suggested Transactional Processes
• Source of light: natural and artificial. • Examples of sources of natural and artificial light.	• Creating situations for sharing personal experiences of children and discussing them. • Demonstrating luminous and non-luminous objects (plain paper and paper with oil drop).

• Luminous/non-luminous objects. • Properties of light. • Transparent, translucent and opaque objects. Examples of each category of objects. • Uses of these objects in daily life. • Formation of shadows (how a shadow is formed-not in technical terms).	• Initiating discussion, asking, questions related to light and its properties, showing simple activities/experiments. • Organizing activities to identify different objects as transparent, translucent and opaque. • Conducting experiments to demonstrate how shadow is formed.

Suggested Learning Resources
- Pictures/live examples of various sources of light.
- Objects depicting transparent, translucent, opaque features.
- Photographs/Pictures on the process of shadow formation.

Integration: Social Studies (Motions of the Earth)

Theme 10: Measurement

The theme 'Measurement' is expected to develop an awareness and understanding of the need for a unit of measurement to explain any object, process and phenomenon. The theme would also discuss various measuring instruments used in daily life. The emphasis of this unit is not only to develop scientific understanding but also to create a functional understanding of measurement in children.

Learning Outcomes:
Children will be able to:
- appreciate the need for measurement of various things/phenomenon;
- identify various instruments used for measurement;
- differentiate various instruments based on their uses in daily life;
- give examples of unit of measurement of some objects;
- cite examples of activities where unit of measurement is required.

Measurement

Key Concepts	Suggested Transactional Processes
• Need for measurement • Examples of measurement in daily life (buying goods, watching time) • Simple description of instruments used for measurement (ruler, tape, weighing machine, thermometer, clock) • Use of each instrument, how to read/use them.	• Providing opportunities for discussion, interaction among peer group; child and teacher. • Creating situations in the classroom for questioning, making questions. • Demonstrating each instrument to observe and describe. • Discussing uses of each instrument in daily life. • Demonstrating 'How to use' with instructions.

Suggested Learning Resources
- Discussion/question answer interaction among children and teacher
- Instruments used for measurement (scale, tape, weighing machine, ruler, clock, etc.)
- Examples/situations where unit of measurement is required
- Children's drawings.

Integration: Mathematics (Measurement)

Theme 11: Push and Pull

In this theme, children will learn that pushes and pulls are examples of Force which can change the shape/ direction of an object. Children will also be familiarized with the various kinds of forces experienced in day-to-day life.

Learning Outcomes:
Children will be able to:
- discuss examples of push and pull seen in day-to-day life;
- differentiate between push and pull and give examples of each;
- describe push and pull in their own words (not definition);
- identify various kind of forces seen in day-to-day life (muscular, gravitational, magnetic, frictional);
- explain each force in their own words; cite examples of each force by relating it with daily life;
- demonstrate push and pull situation in a group activity (with safety precautions).

Push and Pull

Key Concepts	Suggested Transactional Processes
• The concept/ meaning of push and pull and difference between the two; • Examples of push and pull. • Force: meaning in simple terms, changes shape of objects and direction; • Meaning of various types of forces – muscular, gravitational, magnetic and frictional.	• howing and discussing the difference between push and pull and citing examples of each in groups; • Sharing/showing push and pull situations as a demonstration activity and later involving students to do it in groups; • Demonstrating various kinds of forces through simple activities, • Organizing group activities for demonstration of various kinds of forces by children and explaining them in their own words

Suggested Learning Resources
• Apparatus/Objects to demonstrate push and pull
• Pictures of examples of push and pull in real life situations.

Integration: Physical Education.

Theme 12: Friction as a Force

In this theme, children will build on their previous knowledge of Forces and learn more about Friction as a force and the role it plays in our lives. The theme will focus on uses of friction and also on concept formation by using simple examples.

Learning Outcomes:
Children will be able to:
• cite examples of friction observed in daily life and explain friction in their own words;
• explain uses and harmful effects of friction in daily life;
• conduct simple activities/experiments demonstrating friction.

Friction as a Force

Key Concepts	Suggested Transactional Processes
• Friction – meaning, concept. • How to reduce friction (oil, powder). • Uses of friction. • Harmful effects of friction. • Examples of friction.	• Providing opportunities to children to discuss / share their experiences. • Conducting activities / experiments that demonstrate friction. • Creating situations to demonstrate friction on various kinds of surfaces. • Asking children to identify situations where friction may be harmful.

Suggested Learning Resources
• Children's experiences.
• Oil, powder and other objects that can illustrate friction.
• Different surfaces
• Playing Carom Board.

Contents

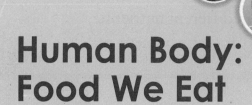

1

Human Body: Food We Eat

Key Concepts

- Food for energy, for work, food for growth (body building), food for protection from diseases.
- Components of food: Carbohydrates, Proteins, Fats, Vitamins, Minerals, Water and roughage as essential components.
- Examples of each group of food component.
- An idea of a balanced diet.
- Care of food to avoid wastage.

 **W**arming up

- Rita likes ice cream and potato chips. She only eats these. Do you think Rita will be healthy? Why? What else do you think she should eat?

WHY DO YOU NEED FOOD?

How do you feel if you do not get food for a long time? Don't you feel weak? You need food to live. All living things need food to live. You need food for the following reasons.

- To get energy to work and play.
- To grow.
- To help you stay healthy by fighting diseases.
- To replace damaged parts of your body. For example when you get hurt, your skin, muscles and even bones may get damaged. Your body replaces the damaged cells with new ones to repair the damage.

Food has special substances in it called nutrients. There are five types of nutrients in food—carbohydrates, proteins, fats, vitamins and minerals. Some nutrients provide energy. Others help you to grow. Some other nutrients help you to fight diseases. Different foods contain different nutrients. That is why you need to eat a variety of food to stay healthy.

Eat variety of food to stay healthy

ENERGY-GIVING FOODS

Foods rich in carbohydrates and fats provide you energy. They are called **energy-giving foods**.

Carbohydrates

Carbohydrates are the nutrients that give you quick energy. Sugar and starches are carbohydrates. Cereals such as rice, wheat and corn are rich in starch. Food prepared from cereal such as boiled rice, chapatti, bread, dosa and idli give you quick energy. Potatoes are also rich in starch. Sweets, chocolates and fruits such as mango and banana are rich in sugar.

Foods containing sugar

Foods containing starch

Fats

Fats are the nutrients that also give you energy. They give you more energy than carbohydrates. The body stores some of the fats you eat for later use. This stored fat is used to get energy whenever the body does not get enough food. Fat also helps to keep you warm.

| Peanuts | Oil | Butter | Cheese |

Foods containing fats

Fats are found in vegetable oils, butter, ghee, nuts, fish and meat.

Your body does not require too much fat to be healthy. Eating too much fat will make your body fat. This is known as **obesity**. It can also cause diseases of the heart when you become older.

BODY-BUILDING FOODS

Foods rich in **proteins** help your body to grow and to replace damaged cells. That is why foods rich in proteins are known as body-building foods. Proteins are found in pulses, fish, meat, milk and milk products, eggs, cereals and nuts. Children need more proteins than adults.

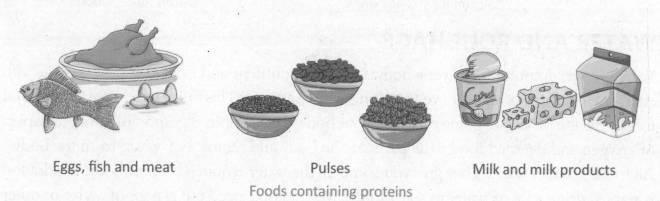

Eggs, fish and meat   Pulses   Milk and milk products

Foods containing proteins

PROTECTIVE FOODS

Foods rich in **vitamins** and **minerals** are called **protective foods**. They are needed in small quantities for good health and proper growth of your body. You need several different kinds of vitamins and minerals. If you do not get any vitamin or mineral in proper quantities, it can cause dangerous diseases.

Vitamins

Some vitamins your body needs are vitamins A, B, C, D, E and K. Vegetables, fruits, nuts, cereals, eggs, fish and chicken are rich in different vitamins.

Vitamin A good for eyesight   Vitamin B good for heart and nerves   Vitamin C good for skin, bones, teeth and gums   Vitamin D good for bones and teeth

Minerals

Some minerals your body needs are iron, calcium, iodine and phosphorus. Green vegetables, fruits, milk, eggs, meat, fish and chicken are rich in different minerals.

Calcium for strong bones   Iron forms blood

WATER AND ROUGHAGE

Water is very important for your body. It is not a nutrient and does not provide you with energy. However, we cannot live very long without water. This is because water is required for several life processes going on inside your body, for example, digestion of food, transport of oxygen and digested food to all parts of the body and removal of waste from the body. All foods contain water. They give you some of the water required by your body. In addition you must drink a lot of water to stay healthy. Most people need 6-8 glasses of water or other liquids every day.

Roughage (or **fibre**) is the part of food that cannot be digested by the body. It is not a nutrient. However, it is important that the food you eat has sufficient roughage. It helps your body get rid of undigested food.

Roughage is present in plant foods. Spinach and cabbage have a lot of roughage.

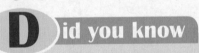

Did you know

A person can live without food for a month but only about a week without water.

A BALANCED DIET

For good health, your diet should have all the nutrients that your body needs in the right quantities. A **balanced diet** consists of the right nutrients in the right amounts.

To help you select a balanced diet, foods have been divided into four groups. These are:

1. **Milk group:** Milk, cheese, curd etc. that give you proteins, fats and minerals.

2. **Protein group:** Meat, eggs, fish, beans, nuts, peas, etc. that give you proteins and fats.

3. **Cereals group:** Rice, bread, chapatti, noodles, etc. that give you carbohydrates and minerals.

4. **Vegetable and fruit group:** Fresh vegetables and fruits that are rich in vitamins, minerals and carbohydrates.

Milk group   Protein group   Cereals group   Fruits and vegetables group

For a balanced diet you need to eat food from each group every day. If you do not eat meat, you should eat more of pulses and dairy food, which will provide you with enough proteins.

REDUCING WASTAGE OF FOOD

Do you sometimes take too much food in your plate and then throw it away?

Whenever you do this remember that there are many children in the world who do not get enough food to eat.

Here are some ways in which you can reduce wastage of food.

- Do not buy too much food at a time. Often people buy more than they need and some of it goes bad.
- Store fruits, vegetables and cooked food properly in the refrigerator.
- Do not take too much food at a time on your plate. You can always take a second helping if you need more. This way you will not waste food.
- If some cooked food is left over and you do not want to eat it, store it in the deep freezer of your refrigerator. You can again take it out after a few days and eat it. Also, leftover food can be used to make other delicious dishes. For example left over vegetables can be used to make sandwiches!

LINKED SITES

An interactive site with games, activities, fun recipes, and a kids panel to help kids learn about healthy eating and staying active.

http://www.nutritionexplorations.org/kids/nutrition-pyramid.asp

Indian calorie chart

http://www.hindustanlink.com/recepiet/indian_calorie_chart.htm

Keywords

Body-building food : Food rich in proteins.
Energy-giving food : Food rich in carbohydrates or fats.
Protective food : Food rich in vitamins and minerals.
Balanced diet : A diet that contains the right nutrients in the right amounts.

Points to Remember

- You need food to get energy, to grow, to fight diseases and to replace damaged parts of your body.
- The nutrients required by the body for good health are: proteins, carbohydrates, fats, vitamins and minerals. Besides these nutrients, water and roughage are also required.
- Carbohydrates and fats are energy-giving foods, proteins are body-building foods, vitamins and minerals are protective foods.
- You must eat a balanced diet, containing all the nutrients that your body needs in proper quantities.
- You should reduce wastage of food

EXERCISE

1. **Fill in the blank boxes with the names of the nutrients and what kind of food each is. One is done for you.**

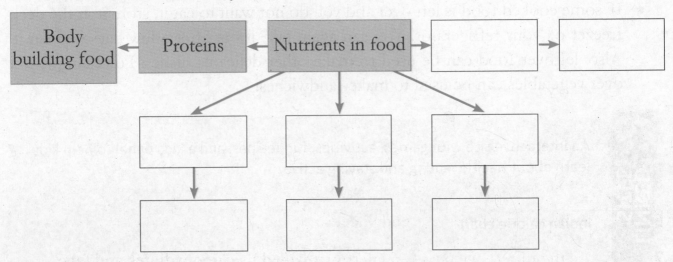

2. **Multiple Choice Questions (MCQs)**

   a. Which of these foods give you energy to store?

      (i) Sweets   (ii) Bread   (iii) Butter   (iv) All of these

   b. Which nutrient helps your body to grow?

      (i) Proteins   (ii) Carbohydrates   (iii) Vitamins   (iv) Fats

   c. Which of these nutrients is very important but required only in very small quantities?

      (i) Proteins   (ii) Carbohydrates   (iii) Vitamins   (iv) Fats

   d. Which of these foods is needed for strong bones?

      (i) Nuts   (ii) Fish   (iii) Bread   (iv) Milk

3. **Name these.**

   a. The food that keeps your body warm. ....

   b. If you do not get them in proper quantities in your food, you can get dangerous diseases. ....

   c. This makes up more than half your body weight. ....

   d. They give you quick energy. ....

   e. Diet that has all the necessary nutrients. ....

   f. Part of food that helps to get rid of undigested food. ....

4. **A. Match the food with the vitamin or mineral it is rich in.**

   B. Write the name of one more food that is rich in the same vitamin or mineral

Column A	Column B	
a. Milk	(i) Vitamin A	....
b. Orange	(ii) Vitamin B	....
c. Fish	(iii) Vitamin C	....
d. Apple	(iv) Vitamin D	....
e. Bread	(v) Iron	....

5. **Why do we need food?**

6. **Name the five nutrients our body needs.**

7. **What is the difference between energy provided by carbohydrates and fats?**

8. What are body-building foods?

9. Water is not a nutrient. But it is important to drink water. Why?

10. What is a balanced diet?

Thinking Questions

1. All nutrients are important for all of us. Which two nutrients are especially important for growing, active children? Why?

Science in everyday life

Many children like eating food such as chips, burgers and fizzy drinks all the time. These foods do not provide a balanced diet. Chips and burgers have excess fat and salt but lack other nutrients. Fizzy drinks have excess sugar and no other nutrient. That is why these are called 'junk food'. You should avoid such food and eat them only occasionally.

Fun to Do

Activity-1

Find out

Different foods give you different amounts of energy. The energy in food can be measured in Calories. An apple gives you about 100 Calories. A 100 gram chocolate bar gives you about 600 Calories.

When you work, you use Calories. The more you run around, the more Calories you use up. You will use up about 100 Calories, if you skip rope for 15 minutes. If you sit all day, you do not use many Calories.

If you eat more Calories than you use up, you have Calories left over. This gets converted to body fat and your weight increases. If you eat a lot, but do very little work, you will get fatter and fatter. Such people can have health problems.

Work in groups to find the number of Calories in different food items. You can consult books, the Internet and dieticians (see linked sites on 19).

Activity-2

Data collection and analysis

Make a list of five fruits – for example, banana, mango, apple, grapes and watermelon. Ask your classmates to write the name of the fruit he/she likes the most on a piece of paper. Collect the papers and count how many like each fruit the most. Fill in the table. Make a bar chart. On the chart mark the 'most liked' and 'least liked' fruits.

	Banana	Mango	Apple	Grape	Watermelon
No. of children who like it the most					

2 Human Body: The Teeth

Key Concepts

- Kind of teeth in the mouth and location.
- Structure and Functions of each kind of tooth.
- Diagram with labelling of parts of a tooth, number of teeth of each kind in: infants and adults.
- Care of Teeth and Gums: Causes of cavities/ deficiencies and steps to prevent them.
- Need for regular check-up to keep teeth healthy; importance of healthy dental care habits.
- Role of food in the development of healthy teeth and gums.

Warming up

- Which is the hardest part of your body?
- What do you think would have happened if it was not so hard?

The hardest part of your body is the surface of your teeth. It has to bear cutting and grinding of food for your whole life. A good set of teeth will make you look nice. They also help you to speak clearly. You must look after them well so that they last a lifetime.

The teeth of a new born baby are hidden below the gums. The baby cannot chew solid food. It can only drink milk and other liquids. When the baby is about six months old, the teeth start appearing. By the time she is about three years old, she has 20 teeth. These teeth are called milk teeth.

At the age of six, the milk teeth start falling out. New teeth appear in their place. These are called permanent teeth. If you look after them well, these teeth will last a lifetime. But if you do not look after them properly, you can lose these teeth. No new teeth will appear in their place.

There are 32 permanent teeth. All of them appear by the age of 21.

KINDS OF TEETH

You know that your teeth cut, tear and grind food. Teeth have special shapes to do these jobs. Look at your teeth in a mirror. Do they have different shapes? What differences can you see between your front teeth and your back teeth?

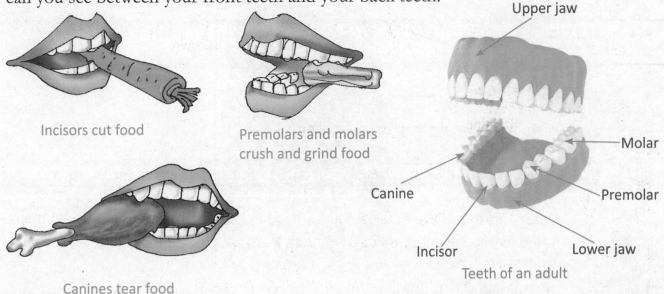

Incisors cut food

Premolars and molars crush and grind food

Canines tear food

Upper jaw

Molar

Canine

Premolar

Incisor

Lower jaw

Teeth of an adult

Your front teeth are your cutting teeth. These are called **incisors**. You have eight incisors, four above and four below.

Next to your cutting teeth are the tearing teeth, called **canines**. You have four **canines**. They are pointed.

The teeth at the back of your mouth crush and grind food. They are wider and flatter than other teeth. These are the **premolars** and **molars**. An adult has eight premolars and twelve molars.

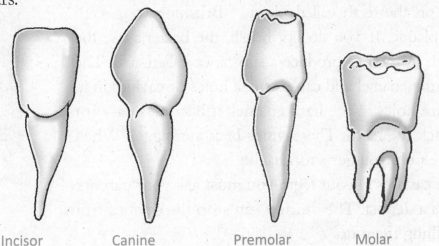

Incisor   Canine   Premolar   Molar

STRUCTURE OF A TOOTH

The part of the tooth above the **gums** is called the **crown**. The part inside the gums is called the **root**. It holds the tooth firmly in place.

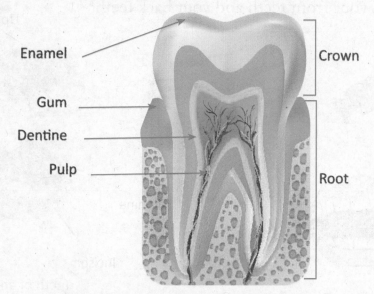

The surface of the crown, known as the **enamel**, is the hardest substance in the human body. Below the enamel is the **dentine**, which is not as hard as the enamel. Inside the dentine is the soft **pulp**. It has blood vessels that provide nutrients to the tooth. It also has nerves.

TAKING CARE OF YOUR TEETH

When you eat, small bits of food get stuck between your teeth. Bacteria present in your mouth mix with the bits of food to form a sticky film on the teeth called **plaque**. Brushing your teeth removes the plaque. If you do not brush, the bacteria use the sugar or starch in food to produce a substance called acid. The acid weakens the enamel and causes small holes or cavities in it. Once there are holes in the hard enamel, it becomes easy for germs to attack the teeth. The cavities become bigger. When they reach the pulp you get a toothache.

Cavity in tooth

If you notice cavities in your teeth you must ask your parents to take you to a dentist. The **dentist** can stop the cavities from growing by filling them up.

To avoid cavities and other teeth problems such as bad breath and diseased gums, make sure that you do the following.

- Brush your teeth twice a day—once in the morning and once at night.
- Rinse your mouth thoroughly after eating or drinking something, especially after eating sugary food.
- Gently massage your gums with your fingers when you brush your teeth.
- Visit a dentist once in six months for a check-up.

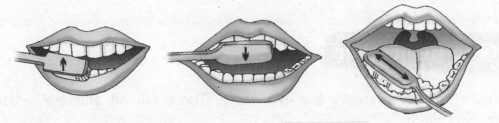

The proper way to brush your teeth

FOODS FOR HEALTHY GUMS AND TEETH

These foods are good for your teeth and gums.

- Foods rich in calcium such as milk, cheese, curd (yoghurt), spinach, broccoli and almonds.
- Foods rich in vitamin D such as fish, egg and tofu. Sitting in the sun for 15-20 minutes a day also provides you with vitamin D.
- Food rich in vitamin C such as lemon, orange, broccoli and strawberry.

The following foods are bad for your teeth and gums and should be avoided. If you do eat them, make sure you rinse your mouth thoroughly after eating.

- Hard or sticky sweets such as candy: such foods stick to your teeth and are not easily washed away.
- Crunchy foods such as potato chips: they get trapped in your teeth and do not easily come out.
- Fizzy cold drinks such as cola: they are harmful for the enamel of your teeth.

LINKED SITES

Watch a fun movie on the teeth:
    https://kidshealth.org/en/kids/teeth-movie.html?ref=search
How much do you know about teeth? Take a quiz:
    https://kidshealth.org/en/kids/teethquiz.html?ref=search

Plaque : A sticky colourless film of bacteria on teeth.

Enamel : The hard white portion of tooth.

Points to Remember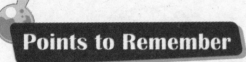

◈ A child's first set of teeth are milk teeth. These fall off and are replaced by the permanent teeth.

◈ We have different kinds of teeth: incisors for cutting, canines for tearing, and premolars and molars for crushing and grinding food.

◈ Teeth consist of the hard enamel, the dentine and the soft pulp.

◈ If teeth are not kept clean, cavities can develop in them.

◈ Sweets, crunchy foods and frizzy drinks should be avoided as they are bad for your teeth and gums.

EXERCISE

1. **This shows the structure of a canine tooth. Label the picture with words from the box.**

Crown, Root, Enamel, Dentine, Pulp, Gum

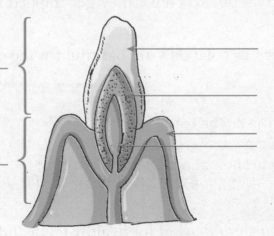

2. **Multiple Choice Questions (MCQs)**

   a. How many teeth does a child of age 3 have?

   (i)   20 milk teeth   (ii)   20 permanent teeth

   (iii) 32 milk teeth   (iv) 32 permanent teeth

   b. The hardest part of teeth is the:

   (i)   Enamel   (ii)   Dentine

   (iii) Pulp   (iv) Gum

   c. Which teeth in your mouth are wide and flat?

   (i)   Incisors   (ii)   Molars

   (iii) Premolars   (iv) Both (ii) and (iii)

   d. You get a toothache when a cavity in the tooth reaches the:

   (i)   Crown   (ii)   Dentine

   (iii) Pulp   (iv) Gum

3. **Put ✓ for true, and ✗ for false.**

   a. The enamel is harder than bones.   ☐

   b. Every time a tooth falls off, a new tooth grows in its place.   ☐

   c. All teeth have the same shape.   ☐

   d. The dentine is the softest part of a tooth.   ☐

   e. Once a cavity is formed in a tooth, it has to be taken out.   ☐

4. **What are each of these useful for?**

   a. Incisors ....

   b. Canines ....

   c. Premolars and molars ....

5. **Name three nutrients that are good for your teeth and one food each in which these nutrients are present.**

6. **Name three foods you should avoid for healthy teeth and gums.**

7. **Use the clues below to find the word in the word grid.**

I	N	F	E	C	T	I	O	U	S	P
D	F	A	C	Z	W	X	Y	M	N	O
M	**M**	I	L	K	T	E	E	T	H	M
O	A	D	H	L	P	Q	V	X	Z	G
P	**C**	R	O	W	N	P	N	**P**	A	E
T	A	P	P	X	Y	O	A	U	C	R
E	N	X	M	N	O	P	Y	L	T	M
R	I	Z	O	A	C	E	G	P	P	S
C	N	M	**D**	E	N	T	I	S	T	C
S	E	O	A	P	L	Y	M	N	O	R
U	S	D	C	V	I	R	U	S	E	S

a. Teeth that fall off and are replaced by new teeth.

b. Tearing teeth.

c. The portion of a tooth above the gums.

d. The portion of the tooth that has blood vessels.

e. The doctor who treats your teeth.

Thinking Questions
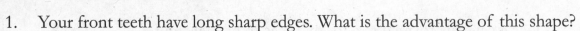

1. Your front teeth have long sharp edges. What is the advantage of this shape?
3. Teeth start paining only when the cavity reaches the pulp. Why?

Science in everyday life

You must take very good care of your teeth so that they last for a lifetime. If cavities or plaque develop in your teeth, you will have to undergo uncomfortable dental procedures like fillings and extractions. Follow the guidelines mentioned in the chapter for a healthy set of teeth.

Fun to Do

Project

Collecting and presenting scientific data

Carry out a survey in your class on the toothpastes used by students. Record your findings in the table below.

Name of toothpaste	Number of students who use it

Draw a bar chart to represent the data.

Which is the most popular toothpaste?

3

Human body: The Digestive and Excretory Systems

Key Concepts

- Organs of the digestive system (mouth, food pipe, stomach, liver, small and large intestine, rectum, anus).
- Functions of various organs in digestion, need for chewing food well, and for regular bowel movements.
- Need for water.
- Organs of the excretory system and their functions.
- Healthy habits related to digestion and excretion.

Warming up

- For food to be used by your body, it must be absorbed by the cells of your body. But food particles are too big to be directly absorbed into the tiny cells. So how do you think they get absorbed?

THE DIGESTIVE SYSTEM

To work properly, every part of your body needs food. Food has to reach your body cells. Here, it is used to provide energy. But before it can enter the cells, it has to be broken down into tiny, simple pieces which can dissolve in water. Breaking down of food inside the body is called digestion.

When you eat food, it goes through your digestive system. This system is a group of body parts that work together to digest the food.

Inside the Mouth

Digestion begins inside the mouth. You first use your teeth to chew food and break it down into small pieces.

The food is mixed with **saliva** and made into a paste before swallowing. Saliva is a digestive juice made by the **salivary glands** present inside your mouth. Saliva softens the food and also starts the digestion of starches in the food. The **tongue** helps to mix the food with the saliva.

Inside the stomach

When you swallow the food, it goes down a tube called the **food pipe** and enters your stomach. It stays there for up to three hours. During this time further digestion of food occurs. The stomach secretes digestive juices. The stomach muscles churn and mix the food with these juices. They break down proteins and other substances into simple soluble substances.

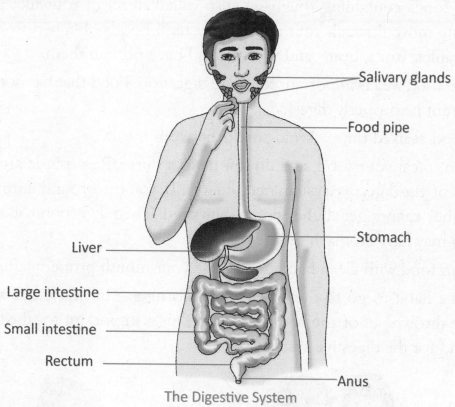

The Digestive System

In the Intestines

From the stomach, the food passes into a coiled pipe called the **small intestine**. Here, the food is mixed with more digestive juices, and it breaks down even more. Some of the digestive juices are made by the small intestine. Some are made by other body organs such as the **liver** and the **pancreas**. The digested food passes into the blood through the walls of the small intestine. The blood takes the digested food to all the cells in the body.

Some portions of the food that you eat cannot be digested. It becomes waste. This passes into a wide pipe called the **large intestine**. Here, water is absorbed from the waste. The solid part or **faeces** is stored in the **rectum** and sent out of the body through the **anus**.

EATING CORRECTLY

- To stay healthy, eat a balanced diet. Too many sweets, or too much of fried food can cause indigestion. Include vegetables, fruits, bread and milk in your diet. Do not eat more than you need, otherwise you will have stomach problems.

- Drink a lot of water. Water helps in the process of digestion.

- Include foods containing roughage (also called fibre) in your diet. It helps food and waste move through your digestive system. Foods obtained from plants such as vegetables, fruits, beans and wheat bread have fibre in them.

- Chewing food well is important for good digestion. Food that has not been chewed well cannot be properly digested.

- Have food at fixed times. Avoid snacks between meals.

- Sit down to eat your food, and do not be in a hurry. Rest a little after eating. The muscles of the digestive system need energy. If you run around during or just after eating, they cannot get all the energy they need. Then digestion will not be proper, and you may have stomach problems.

- Eat clean food with clean hands, and rinse your mouth properly after eating.

- Make it a habit to go to the toilet every morning. The waste left after digestion must be thrown out of the body regularly. This is important for the health of your body and for the digestive system.

THE EXCRETORY SYSTEM

As the body parts do their work, waste materials are produced. For example, when food is converted into energy, carbon dioxide is produced as waste. Other waste materials are also produced. They must be removed from the body otherwise they will harm the body.

Excretion is the process of getting rid of these waste products from the body. The main system in the body responsible for excretion is the **urinary system**. It removes most of the wastes from the body in the form of urine. Other excretory organs are the **skin** and **lungs**. The skin removes waste in the form of sweat and the lungs remove carbon dioxide.

The Urinary System

The main organs of the urinary system are the two bean-shaped organs called **kidneys**. They can be called the filters of the body. The blood collects waste materials from the cells in all parts of the body and takes them to the kidneys. The kidneys filter out these waste materials from the blood.

The waste leaves the kidneys, along with water, through two tubes. They are collected as urine in a bag called the **urinary bladder**. The urine is expelled from time to time.

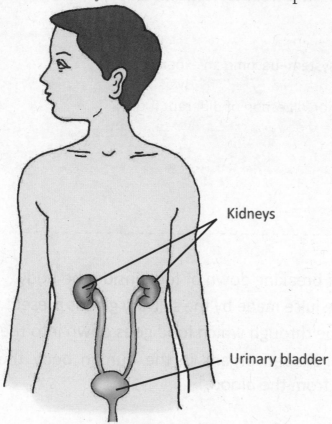

Kidneys

Urinary bladder

The Urinary System

Keeping Your Excretory Organs Healthy

1. Drink plenty of water. Water helps the body in excretion.
2. Exercise daily.

3. Eat a healthy diet. Some foods that provide the nutrients necessary to keep the excretory organs healthy are fruits, vegetables, whole grains, milk and milk products.
4. Go to the toilet when you feel the need - do not hold back your urine.

LINKED SITES

The digestive system—become an expert!
http://kidshealth.org/en/kids/digestive-system.html?WT.ac=en-k-slpmsh-k-lt
Watch a video on digestion of different foods.
http://kitses.com/animation/digestion.html

Keywords

Digestion : Process of breaking down of food inside the body.

Saliva : A digestive juice made by the salivary glands present inside your mouth.

Food pipe : A long tube through which food goes down into the stomach.

Kidneys : Two bean-shaped organs in the human body that filter out waste materials from the blood.

Points to Remember

◈ Food has to be digested before it can be used by the body.

◈ Digestion takes place in the mouth, stomach, and small intestine.

◈ The leftover waste material in food is passed out of the body through the anus.

◈ Having the right eating habits is important for good health.

◈ Excretion is the process of getting rid of waste products of the body.

◈ The urinary system is the main excretory system of the body.

EXERCISE

1. **Label the parts of the digestive system marked in the picture.**

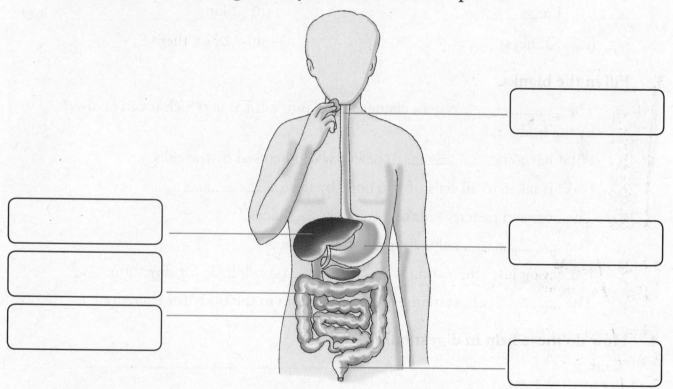

2. **Multiple Choice Questions (MCQs)**

   a. Which of these does saliva help in?

   (i) Softening the food

   (ii) Digestion of starch

   (iii) Removing waste

   (iv) Both (i) and (ii)

b. Where is the digested food absorbed into the blood?

    (i) Stomach   (ii) Small intestine

    (iii) Large intestine   (iv) Mouth

c. Where is water absorbed from the food?

    (i) Stomach   (ii) Food pipe

    (iii) Small intestine   (iv) Large intestine

d. Which of these cannot be digested by the digestive system?

    (i) Vegetables   (ii) Sweets

    (iii) Meat   (iv) Fibre

e. Where does the process of digestion of food begin?

    (i) Mouth   (ii) Food pipe

    (iii) Stomach   (iv) Small intestine

f. Which of these excretory organs filter out waste materials from the blood?

    (i) Lungs   (ii) Skin

    (iii) Kidneys   (iv) All of them

3. Fill in the blanks.

a. The .... system changes food into a form in which it can be used by the body.

b. Food has to be .... before it can be used by the cells.

c. Food is taken to all cells of the body by the ....

d. The liver and pancreas make .... juices.

e. The .... helps to mix food with saliva.

f. Exercising just after eating is .... (good/bad) for digestion.

g. The .... system is the main system in the body for excretion.

4. How do these help in digestion?

Teeth : ....

Saliva : ....

Liver : ....

Digestive juices : ....

Fibre : ....

5. What happens to the food in the small intestine?

6. What happens to the undigested portion of food?

7. Why is excretion necessary?

8. Name two waste products that must be removed from the body.

Thinking Questions

1. Fibre cannot be digested. Therefore it is best to remove all fibre from food before eating. Do you agree? Give reason.

2. A small baby cannot eat any solid food. Why?

3. An athlete thinks that if she eats a lot before a race, her body will get a lot of energy for the race. Do you agree with her? Why?

Science in everyday life

Think!

Do you eat the right kind of food – is your diet balanced?

Do you follow all good eating practices mentioned in the chapter?

Fun to Do

Activity-1

Science experiment

You know that saliva starts the digestion of starch in your food. It turns starch into sugar. Can you taste this sugar? Try it out.

1. Take a slice of white bread.

2. Bite a big piece and chew it for several minutes. You will feel like swallowing it after some time but do not do so. Just keep chewing it for 5-6 minutes.

3. Pay attention to the taste of the bread. Does it change after a few minutes?

Find out :

What happens to food inside the cells?

In steam engines there is a furnace. Coal is the fuel that is burnt in the furnace to give energy. The cells in your body are also like small furnaces. Food is like fuel. To give energy, food must be 'burnt' in the cells. There is, of course, one important difference. In an engine furnace, a lot of heat is produced. In the cells, very little heat is produced while burning food; otherwise, your body would burn up in no time!

You know that burning requires oxygen. Therefore to 'burn' food and produce energy oxygen must reach the cells too.

Find out how oxygen and digested food reach the body cells.

Activity-3

Removal of undigested food from the body from the anus is not considered part of excretion. Find out why.

4 Adaptations in Animals

Key Concepts

- Adaptation in animals.
- Need for adaptations in animals.
- Reasons of adaptations.
- Examples of adaptations in animals: on land, in water.
- Adaption in modification of body parts in herbivores, carnivores, omnivores.
- Examples of each.
- Care and concern for animals

Warming up

- Suppose a polar bear is brought from the cold places where it lives, to a desert. What problems do you think it would have?

PLANTS AND ANIMALS LIVE IN MANY DIFFERENT PLACES

All plants and animals need certain basic things to survive. Plants need water, minerals, sunlight and air. They also need protection from enemies. Animals need food and water, air, warmth, a place to live, and protection from enemies.

A desert scene

Animals and plants live in many different places — in the plains, on mountains, in deserts, in lakes and rivers, in the oceans, and in other places. Weather, soil and other conditions in these different places are different.Plants and animals are adapted to live in these conditions. That is why, plants and animals living in these different conditions are different from one another. As an example, a tiger cannot live in a desert, whereas a camel can. The camel is adapted to the life in a desert where there is very little food. It has a hump on its back where fat is stored. That is why it can stay without food for several days. A tiger does not have any such adaptation and cannot live in the desert.

ADAPTED TO THE SURROUNDINGS

Animals live everywhere on the earth. They live deep inside the oceans where it is totally dark, and also on high mountains which are always covered with snow. Animals living in different places are different from each other. Let us see how they are adapted to their surroundings.

Animals can be divided into five groups according to where they live.

- **Terrestrial** animals live on land.
- **Aquatic** animals live in water.
- **Amphibians** live on both land and water.
- **Arboreal** animals live on trees.
- **Aerial** animals spend most of their time in air.

Terrestrial animals: The bodies of terrestrial animals are suited for life on land. Most of them have legs. They help them run fast to catch their prey or escape from enemies.

How a cheetah moves

Animals like snake have scales which help them to crawl.

How a snake moves

Animals living in cold regions have fur on their bodies to protect them from cold. Animals living in deserts have thick skin which protects them from the sun. It also prevents water loss from their bodies.

Polar bear has fur on its body   Camel has a thick skin

Most land animals have lungs to breathe air. Their senses are well developed. They help them to look for food and escape from enemies.

Some land animals such as lizards and snakes cannot bear cold weather. To survive, they eat a lot of food and then go to sleep in caves or holes under the ground during the winter months. This is called **hibernation**.

Dormouse hibernating

Crab

Fish

Aquatic animals: Fish, crabs, turtles and shrimps live in water. They swim with the help of their tails or special legs. Many breathe air dissolved in water through gills.

Amphibians: Frogs, toads, turtles newts and salamanders live both on land and in water. They have legs that enable them to move on land, and also swim in water. When in water, they breathe through their skin. They also have lungs which help them to breathe when on land. Frogs hibernate in cold weather.

Frog   Salamander   Turtle   Newt

Arboreal animals: Monkeys, squirrels and garden lizards are some animals that live on land but spend a lot of their time on trees. They have claws, strong arms and legs which help them to climb trees. Monkeys swing from branch to branch and use their tails to balance themselves and grip the branches.

Monkey   Squirrel

Aerial animals: Many birds and bats spend most of their time in the air. They have wings to fly. They have light bodies covered with feathers. Their bones are hollow and light. Their bodies are shaped like aeroplanes. All these are adaptations that make it easy for them to fly. Insects such as butterflies, wasp and bees are also aerial animals. Bats are the only mammals that can fly.

Bat (Mammal)

Eagle (Bird)

Wasp (Insect)

Many birds living in very cold places such as Siberia cannot survive the cold winter there. So they fly thousands of kilometres to warmer places in winter in search of food and shelter. They go back when the winter ends. This is called **migration**. Several birds migrate to India in winters.

Migration

ADAPTATIONS TO THE KIND OF FOOD EATEN

Animals eat plants or other animals. They can be divided into four groups according to the food they eat.

Herbivores are animals that eat plants. Buffaloes, cows, deer and horses are herbivores (or herbivorous animals). They have sharp cutting teeth in front and flat grinding teeth at the back.

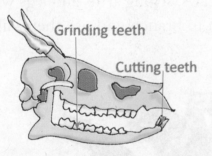
Grinding teeth
Cutting teeth
Teeth of a deer

Deer

Horse

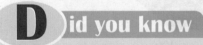
Did you know

A giraffe tongue is so long that it uses it to clean its ears.

Carnivores are animals that eat the flesh of other animals. Lions, tigers, foxes, dogs, snakes, eagles and vultures are some carnivores (or carnivorous animals). These animals have long, sharp teeth or beaks to tear the flesh. Snakes swallow their prey whole. Some carnivores such as lions or tigers kill and eat other animals. They are very strong and can run very fast. Other carnivores such as jackal eat the flesh of dead animals.

Tiger (a carnivore)   Teeth of a tiger

Omnivores are animals that eat both plants and animals. Bears, crows and cockroaches are omnivorous animals. Humans are also omnivores. Since bears and humans eat both plants and animals, they have a combination of sharp front teeth, pointed teeth and flat teeth.

Crow   Cockroach
Omnivorous animals

Parasites are small animals that depend on other living animals for their food. Mosquitoes, which suck the blood of humans and other animals, are parasites. Instead of teeth they have a long sharp pipe. They stab animals with this pipe and suck their blood like we drink cold drinks with a straw. Fleas, leeches and bugs are also parasites. They live on the bodies of animals and suck their blood.

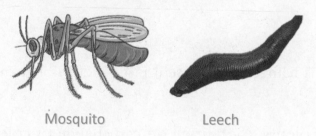

Mosquito   Leech

Some parasites such as hookworm, roundworm and tapeworm live inside the bodies of humans and other animals. They eat the food after it has been digested by the animal.

 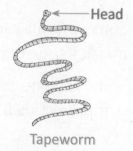

Head

Roundworms   Tapeworm

ADAPTATIONS FOR PROTECTION

Animals have adaptations to protect themselves from being eaten by other animals.

Some animals can run or fly away very fast. A mouse protects itself from a cat by running fast and hiding in small places. A bird protects itself by flying away. A deer can run very fast to escape from a lion. The ocean has many kinds of fish. Big fish such as sharks eat the smaller fish. A small fish called puffer fish protects itself by puffing up like a balloon. This makes the sharp spines on its body poke out. The shark cannot eat it.

Spines

Puffer fish

The colour and shape of some animals are such that they merge with the surroundings. This is called **camouflage**. Camouflage makes an animal hard to see.

A polar bear lives in very cold places. Its white fur matches the snow. The stick insect looks like a twig and is difficult to make out when it is sitting on a plant. Zebras, tigers and leopards have spots or stripes on their bodies which match with their surroundings in the forests. This makes it difficult to see them.

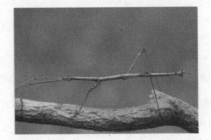

Stick insect
(Can you see the insect?)

Zebra

Leopard

Did you know

The Elephant grass found in Africa is named so because it is 4.5 meters high and even elephants can hide in it !

Some animals can also change their colours. **A chameleon** can change its colour to match its surroundings.

Some animals defend themselves with **shells and spines**. Turtles and snails have shells that protect their soft bodies. Other animals such as porcupine have sharp spines.

Spines

Hard shell

Porcupine

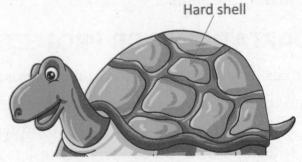

Tortoise

CARE AND CONCERN FOR ANIMALS

Animals are a wonderful part of our lives. They give us love. They bring us a lot of joy and make us laugh. We should respect them and be kind to them.

- Never tease or hit animals.
- If you have a pet at home, make sure that it is regularly cleaned and gets clean food and water. Also, see that the place it lives in, is kept clean.
- If there is an animal shelter near your house visit it regularly to work for the animals and give them company.

LINKED SITES

Lots to see and learn on this BBC animals site.
http://www.bbc.co.uk/nature/animals/
Lots of activities and games on animals
http://www.sciencekids.co.nz/animals.html

Keywords

Migration : Going to far off places to escape the cold winters, and returning in summers
Hibernation : Sleeping throughout winters to escape from cold.

Points to Remember

- Plants and animals are adapted to the conditions in which they live.
- Animals are adapted to their surroundings, to the kind of food they eat and to protect themselves from enemies.
- Animals can be grouped as terrestrial, aquatic, amphibian, arboreal or aerial according to where they live.
- Animals can be grouped as herbivores, carnivores, omnivores or parasites, according to the food they eat.
- Animals have different adaptations to protect themselves from being eaten by other animals.
- We should respect animals and be kind to them.

1. Fill in the blank boxes in this mind map of where animals live.

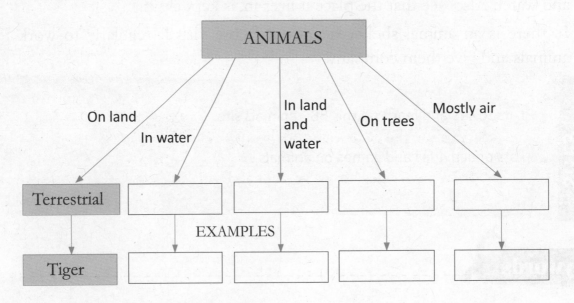

ANIMALS

On land

In water

In land and water

On trees

Mostly air

Terrestrial

EXAMPLES

Tiger

2. Multiple Choice Questions(MCQs)

a. Most land animals breathe with the help of their:

   (i) Lungs

   (ii) Gills

   (iii) Skin

   (iv) Stomata

b. What is common between these animals – frog, newt, salamander?

   (i) They breathe only through lungs.

   (ii) They breathe only through gills.

   (iii) They breathe through lungs and gills.

   (iv) They breathe through lungs and skin.

c. Humans are:

   (i) Herbivores

   (ii) Carnivores

   (iii) Omnivores

   (iv) Parasites

d. Migration means:

   (i) Hunting for food during the day and coming home at night

   (ii) Hunting for food at night and coming home at sunrise

   (iii) Going to far off places to escape from cold winters, and returning in summers

   (iv) Going to sleep in winters to escape from cold

e. Which of these animals lives inside the bodies of other animals?

    (i) Mosquito   (ii) Roundworm

    (iii) Leech   (iv) All of these

f. Which of these relies on camouflage?

    (i) Polar bear   (ii) Stick insect

    (iii) Zebra   (iv) All of these

3. Fill in the blanks

1. Roundworm and tapeworm live .... the bodies of humans and other animals.

2. .... are the only mammals that can fly.

3. Snake have .... which help them to crawl.

4. .... have harp cutting teeth in front and flat grinding teeth at the back.

5. We should .... animals and be kind to them .

4. Match the columns.

Column A	Column B
a. A terrestrial animal that does not have legs.	(i) Bird
b. An animal that can breathe through its skin.	(ii) Mosquito
c. An animal whose tail helps it to move around.	(iii) Snake
d. An animal that has hollow bones.	(iv) Chameleon
e. An animal that sucks the blood of other animals.	(v) Toad
f. An animal that can change colour.	(vi) Monkey

5. Why is it necessary for animals to adapt themselves to the surroundings?

6. What do the following mean?

a. Aquatic animals   ....

b. Arboreal animals   ....

c. Aerial animals   ....

d. Amphibians   ....

e. Parasites   ....

7. How are the teeth of these animals adapted to suit the food they eat?

   a. Herbivores   b. Carnivores

8. Describe any two ways in which animals protect themselves.

9. List the adaptations found in aerial animals.

Thinking Questions

1. A tiger uses camouflage to hide in grass. However a tiger does not require camouflage for protection. Then how does this camouflage help the tiger?

2. A tapeworm does not have a well-developed digestive system. Why does it not need it?

3. What problems will a polar bear have if it is left in a desert?

Science in everyday life

The air in places very high above sea level is thin. If you go to such a place, for example Ladakh, you will have difficulty in breathing and cannot do much activity. You are advised to rest for 1-2 days. After that your body gets adapted to the thin air, and you can breathe properly. So if your family plans a trip to such a place you should keep an additional 1-2 days to get adapted to the conditions there.

Fun to Do

Project 1

Find out and write a report

How did the dinosaurs die?

Huge dinosaurs lived on this earth, millions of years ago, before humans lived on the Earth. They all died about 65,000,000 years ago. No one knows for sure why they died, but there are different ideas.

Some scientists believe that when small animals appeared on the Earth, they ate eggs of dinosaurs. The dinosaurs were not able to protect their eggs and so they slowly disappeared.

Find out about some other ideas that scientists have given. Write a report.

All ideas have one thing in common.

There was some change in the surroundings in which the dinosaurs lived. They were not adapted to survive in the changed conditions and died.

Project 2

Find out :

Animals in Danger

Today humans are cutting down forests for farming and for making cities. This results in many animals losing their homes. Some animals are being killed for their body parts. Crocodiles and snakes are killed for their skin, and elephants for their tusks.

The government is now taking several steps to protect animals. Killing of several animals is not allowed. Wildlife parks (or sanctuaries) have been made to protect animals such as tigers.

Find out about the wildlife sanctuaries in India. Find out what laws have been made by the government to protect animals. You can meet an officer of a zoo or a wildlife sanctuary to find this out.

The map on the next page shows the wildlife sanctuaries in India to save the tiger.

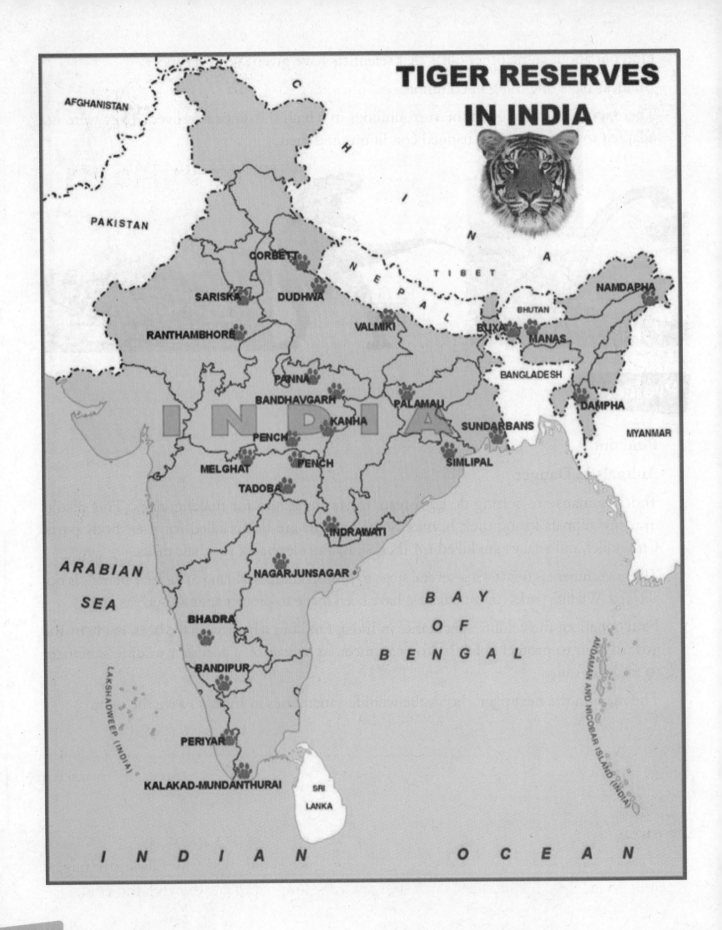

TIGER RESERVES IN INDIA

5

Adaptations in Plants

- Need for adaptation in plants.
- Examples of adaptation of plants on land with examples.
- Examples of adaptation of plants in water with examples.
- Examples of adaptation of plants in desert with examples.
- Examples of adaptation of plants in hilly areas with examples.

Warming up

- You saw in Chapter 4 that animals are adapted to the kind of environment they live in. Do you think plants are also adapted to the environment they live in?
- Compare a cactus plant with a lotus plant. What differences do you find? Why do you think these differences are there?

The lotus plant grows in the water. It cannot survive in a desert where there is very little water. However, a cactus is adapted to live in a desert. It has a fleshy stem that stores water.

ADAPTATIONS IN LAND PLANTS

Most plants grow on land. They are called terrestrial plants. Some grow in mountains where it is cold. Others grow in deserts. Some grow along the sea coast, and some in places where it is hot and wet.

On mountains

In the cold, hilly areas such as Ooty or Kashmir, trees are generally tall and straight. Many of them have needle-like leaves that are very tough and can survive the cold.

Instead of flowers, they bear **cones** and are therefore called **conifers**. Seeds develop in these cones. Pine, fir, deodar and spruce are examples of such trees. These trees have a strong smell that keeps insects away, and protects the trees from them. They have a sloping shape which enables snow to slip off easily.

Cone and needle-like leaves   A spruce tree

In the plains

Trees such as mango, peepal, banyan and shesham grow in the warmer climate of the plains. They shed their leaves in winter to protect themselves from the cold weather. These trees are called **deciduous** trees.

Coconut and teak trees grow in hot and wet places. They are **evergreen** trees. They do not shed their leaves. Rubber, sugarcane and pepper also grow in such a climate.

Banyan tree   Coconut   Sugarcane

In the deserts

In deserts there is very little water. Plants, therefore, should be adapted to get whatever little water is available. You have already seen how the fleshy stem of cactus stores water. When it rains, the roots absorb water and move it to the stem. The roots

Spreading roots of cactus   Deep roots of mesquite bush

of cactus spread out over a large area. The stem soaks up water like a sponge. The leaves of cactus are shaped like spines. Very little water is lost through such narrow leaves into the air.

Other desert plants such as mesquite bush have roots that go deep down. They can reach water that is 30 metres underground.

In marshes

Some places are marshy. They have clayey soil. There is always a lot of water in the soil. Mangrove trees grow in such soils. Their roots cannot get air in the soil. They have **breathing roots** that grow above the soil. This is how the mangrove trees adapt themselves and survive in their peculiar surroundings.

Breathing roots of mangrove trees

ADAPTATIONS IN WATER PLANTS

A number of plants grow in water, too. These are called aquatic plants. There are three kinds of aquatic plants – those which float on water, those which are fixed, and those which live under water.

Water hyacinth (Floating plant)

Water lily (Fixed plant)

Floating plants are light. They have swollen or spongy bodies. Water hyacinth and duckweed are two such plants.

Fixed plants such as lotus and water lily have roots that fix them to the bed of the pond. They have long hollow stems which are very light. They have broad leaves that float on the surface of water. The stomata are on the upper side of the leaves.

Underwater plants have narrow leaves with no stomata. They breathe through their body surface. Pond weed and tape grass are examples of such plants.

Tape grass
(Underwater plant)

PLANTS – ADAPTATIONS FOR GETTING FOOD

You know that green plants make their own food. Some living things that look-like plants but do not have the green **chlorophyll** required to make food, are called **fungi**. They grow on living plants, on dead plants and animals and on stale food. They get their food from whatever they grow on. Moulds (that grow on stale bread) and mushrooms are examples of fungi.

Fungus growing on a tree

Mushroom

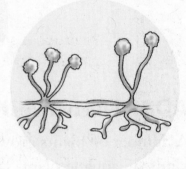

Mould

Some plants even eat insects. The venus flytrap grows in soil that is poor in minerals. It is able to survive in poor soil by catching insects and absorbing their soft parts. The pitcher plant is another example.

Pitcher plant

Venus flytrap

PLANTS – ADAPTATIONS FOR PROTECTION

A number of plants such as cactus and rose have spines on their bodies. This protects them from animals.

Many plants have poisons in them. If you touch poison ivy, your skin will start itching. This keeps animals away.

Some plants which grow in very cold places do not freeze even when snow covers them. They produce a liquid which prevents freezing.

Spines on a cactus plant

Poison ivy

LINKED SITES

Read about and see pictures of adaptations in plants growing in the desert—prepared for a TV show.
http://www.alongtheway.org/plant/plant.html

Get more detailed information about the pitcher plant:

Go to the following site → click on 'ecology' → click on 'Plants' → go to page 4 → click on 'Pitcher plant'
http://www.dimdima.com

You can explore the other links too.

Keywords

Terrestrial plants	:	Plants that grow on land
Aquatic plants	:	Plants that grow in water
Conifers	:	Plants that bear cones
Evergreen trees	:	Trees that do not shed their leaves

Points to Remember

◈ Plants are adapted to their surroundings.

◈ Terrestrial plants are adapted to the conditions in which they grow.

◈ Aquatic plants have body parts that help them to float or to stay under water.

◈ Some plants get their food from other plants and animals.

◈ Plants protect themselves in different ways.

EXERCISE

1. **Fill in the blank boxes in the mind map of terrestrial and aquatic plants.**

   a.

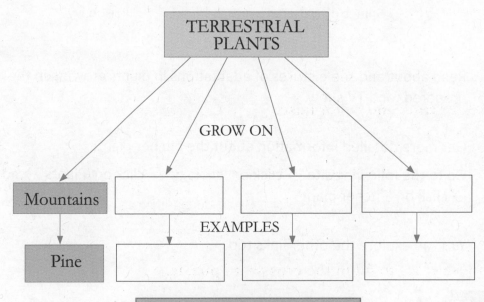

   b.

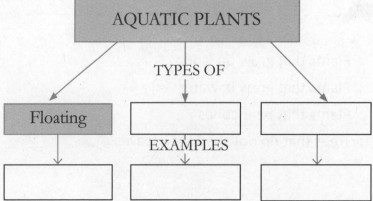

2. **Multiple Choice Questions (MCQs)**

a. In which of these environments will you find a conifer?

    (i) Desert   (ii) Mountain

    (iii) Water   (iv) Hot and wet forests

b. Which of these plants have narrow leaves with no stomata?

    (i) Water lily   (ii) Pine

    (iii) Water hyacinth   (iv) Tape grass

c. Plants growing in which of these environments have roots that grow above the soil to breathe?

    (i) Deserts   (ii) Marshy land

    (iii) Mountains   (iv) Under water

d. Which plants have stomata on the upper surface of leaves?

    (i) Plants that float on water

    (ii) Plants fixed to soil under water but with leaves that float on water

    (iii) Underwater plants

    (iv) All of these

e. Which of following plants traps and eats insects?

    (i) Cactus   (iii) Mushroom

    (iii) Pitcher plant   (iv) Mesquite bush

3. **Put ✓ for true, and ✗ for false.**

a. Some terrestrial plants grow in water

b. The cactus plant stores water in its stem.

c. All desert plants have roots that go very deep in the ground in search of water.

d. Spines protect plants from animals.

4. **Use these clues to fill in the crossword puzzle.**

a. Plants growing on land.

b. Plants that do not shed their leaves in winter

c. Some plants have them instead of flowers.

d. Plant-like living things that cannot make their own food.

e. Place where a mesquite bush is normally found.

5. **Where are these plants normally found?**

    a.   Mango   ....   b. Coconut ....

    c.   Mangrove ....   d. Lotus   ....

    e.   Pine   ....   f. Banyan ....

6. **Name two plants in each case.**

    a.   Cone-bearing plants.   ....

    b.   Plants that protect themselves with spines.   ....

    c.   Plants that catch insects.   ....

    d.   Fungi.   ....

7. **Why do some trees lose their leaves in winter?**

8. **Why do roots of trees growing in marshy land have difficulty in getting air?**

Thinking Questions

1. Leaves of most plants have stomata on their lower surface. Why do leaves of lotus and water lily have stomata on their upper surface?

2. Why do underwater plants have long thin leaves?

3. Can a banyan tree grow well in the cold climate of the mountains?

Fun to Do

Activity-1

Find out :

Medicine from fungus

Fungi, that appear to be so useless are actually our life savers. Some very important medicines are made from fungi.

In 1928, Sir Alexander Fleming, from Scotland, made a chance discovery that changed the treatment of diseases. He was growing bacteria

in a dish. He noticed that a mould had grown in a corner. He was surprised to find that it had killed the bacteria near it. He studied the mould and discovered that it made a substance that could kill bacteria. He called the substance penicillin. It is now used to treat a number of diseases.

Penicillin is called an **antibiotic**. Other such antibiotics made by other kinds of fungi are also now available as medicines.

In 1945, Sir Alexander Fleming and two other scientists who had worked with him, were awarded the Nobel Prize for medicine.

Do you know what the Nobel Prize is? Find out from your teacher or parents. Also find out which Indians have got this award.

Project 1

Science Experiment

Grow mould

You can grow mould on a piece of bread. Take a slice of bread.

Put some dust and a few drops of water on it. Cover it.

After one or two days you will find mould growing on it. Look at it with a magnifying glass. Draw its picture.

Remember to wash your hands afterwards.

6

Plants in the Surroundings and Environment

Key Concepts

- Parts of plants and their uses.
- Roots: kinds of roots, their functions and examples.
- Shoots: functions of the stem.
- Functions of the leaf: Photosynthesis, transpiration process (in simple language).
- Iodine test for starch in leaves.
- Products obtained from plants such as food items, wood, coir, rubber, fibres.

Warming up

- Name some parts of your body. Now look carefully at an animal such as a dog. Which parts of the body of a dog are similar to yours? Which parts are different? Now look carefully at a flowering plant such as rose. Which parts of the body of the rose plant are similar to yours? Which parts are different?
- Is your body more similar to the body of a dog, or to the body of a rose plant?

Your body is made up of several parts. Each part has its own work to do. The bodies of other living beings also have several parts. Let us see what the different parts of a plant are. Let us also see what work each part does.

You already know that a portion of the plant grows above the ground. This is the shoot. The portion that grows below the soil is the root.

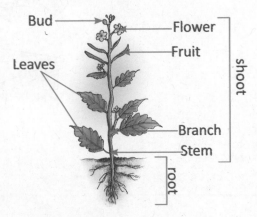

Parts of a plant

THE ROOT

Roots are of different kinds. Some plants have thick roots that go deep into the soil. Other plants have a number of thin, short roots.

There are two main kinds of roots – **tap roots** and **fibrous roots**.

In a tap root, there is a main thick root growing from the end of the stem. Several thinner roots grow from the main root. Plants like bean, pea, balsam and mustard have taproots.

In a fibrous root, a number of equal-sized roots grow from the end of the stem. There is no main root. Grass, wheat, rice and onion have fibrous roots.

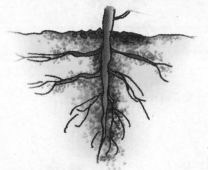
Tap root

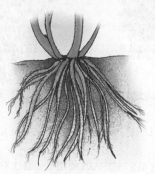
Fibrous root

Functions of the Root

- Roots fix a plant firmly to the soil.
- Roots help the plant take water and minerals from the soil.
- In some plants, such as carrot, radish and beetroot, the food prepared by the plant is stored in the root. We eat these roots.

Carrot

Beetroot

Radish

Roots that store food

THE SHOOT

The shoot has the **stem**, **branches**, **leaves**, **buds**, **flowers** and **fruits**. Fruits have **seeds** inside them. New plants grow from these seeds.

The Stem

The stem supports the plant above the ground. Branches, leaves, buds, fruits and flowers grow on it.

Trees usually have hard, woody, strong stems. The stems are covered with thick bark. Such a stem is called a **trunk**.

Bushes such as rose and hibiscus have thin and hard stems. Herbs such as tomato and mint have soft, green stems.

Mango tree

Rose plant

Tomato plant

Creepers such as strawberry and climbers such as money plant have weak stems. They cannot hold the plant upright. Creepers spread on the ground and climbers need support to climb.

Pumpkin (creeper)

Money plant (climber)

Functions of the Stem

- The stem gives support to the plant above the ground.
- The water taken in by the root of the plant travels to all parts of the plant including the leaves through the stem. Leaves use this water to make food.
- The food made by the leaves is required by all parts of the plant. It travels through the stem to all the parts.
- Sometimes, the food made by the leaves is stored in the stem, as in sugarcane. Potato and ginger are also stems that store food. They are underground stems. We eat these stems.

Potato

Ginger

Sugarcane

Underground Stems

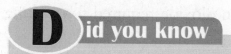
The Leaf

Leaves are of many different shapes and sizes but they are mostly green in colour. The flat part of a leaf is called the **leaf blade**.

The **main vein** or **midrib** is a thin tube that runs through the middle of the leaf. The **side veins** are thinner tubes that come out of the midrib and spread throughout the leaf blade. It is through these veins that water is carried to the leaf. They also carry food from the leaf to all parts of the plant.

The leaf blade has tiny openings on its underside called **stomata** (singular: stoma). The plant takes in and gives out air through the stomata. Excess water is also given out through the stomata.

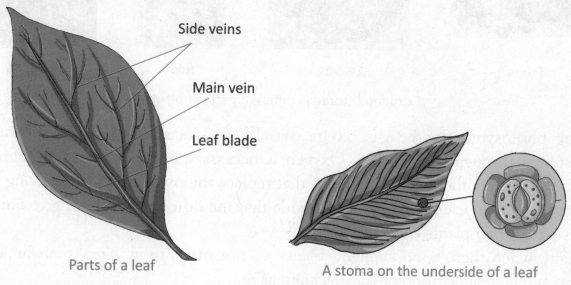

Side veins

Main vein

Leaf blade

Parts of a leaf

A stoma on the underside of a leaf

Functions of the Leaf

A leaf makes food for the plant. In fact, plants make food for the entire living world in their leaves. Plants are the only living things that make food from non-living things.

PHOTOSYNTHESIS – THE PROCESS OF MAKING FOOD

Leaves are mostly green in colour because of a substance called **chlorophyll**. Chlorophyll is necessary for the leaf to make food. That is why only green plants can make food.

The leaf puts together **carbon dioxide** from the air, and **water** from the soil to make food.

- **Air** enters the leaf through the stomata. The carbon dioxide required for making food is absorbed by the leaf from air.
- **Water** taken from the soil reaches the leaf through the stem, main vein and side veins.
- The **energy** which the leaf needs to make food is obtained from sunlight. It is the chlorophyll which absorbs sunlight for this purpose.

This process by which food is made in the leaves is called **photosynthesis**. 'Photo' means light and 'synthesis' means putting together.

During the process of photosynthesis, the food that the leaf prepares is a kind of sugar called **glucose**. The glucose may further change into **starch** before the plant stores it in fruits, stem, roots or leaves.

Fruits

Leaves

Roots

Stems

Extra food stored in different parts of plants

During photosynthesis, the gas **oxygen** is also produced. It is given off into the atmosphere through the stomata. Oxygen is necessary for all plants and animals to breathe. Plants are the only living things that replace the oxygen that other living things use up. They also use up the carbon dioxide that the other living things give out. That is why we say that plants clean the air.

At night, when there is no sunlight, plants do not make food. They then breathe in oxygen and give out carbon dioxide as animals do.

How Plants Use Food

Plants need food like animals do. But they prepare more food than is needed by them.

1. Plants need energy to grow, and to produce flowers, fruits, seeds and more leaves. This energy is provided by the food they prepare.
2. Food is used for growth and to repair damage. For example, if an animal eats a portion of a plant, the plant can make new body parts to repair the damage.
3. The extra food prepared by the plant is stored in different parts such as fruit, stem, root, seed or leaf. Humans and other animals eat this food.

TRANSPIRATION – RELEASING WATER VAPOUR

Another function of the leaf is to release extra water in the form of water vapour. This is called **transpiration**. The water vapour is released from the stomata in the leaf.

Transpiration helps in cooling down the plant. Also, as the water goes out from the leaves, the roots pull more water from the soil and send it to the leaves. This water brings with it nutrients from the soil which are required by the plant.

You can do a simple experiment to study transpiration.

1. Take a small potted plant and water it.

2. Cover it with a transparent plastic bag. Tie the mouth of the bag.

3. Keep the plant in the sun.

4. Observe after a few hours. Can you see water droplets in the plastic bag?

   Where did the water vapour come from?

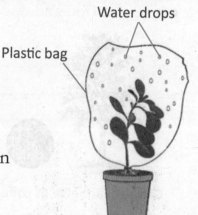

Water drops

Plastic bag

PLANT PRODUCTS

Food: We get many kinds of food items from plants.

- Many kinds of **fruits**, **vegetables**, **grains** and **pulses** (*dals*)

Vegetables

Fruits

- **Oils** such as groundnut oil, coconut oil, sunflower oil and mustard oil.

Mustard oil

Coconut oil

- **Spices** such as pepper, turmeric (*haldi*), clove and cardamom.

Spices

- **Tea**, **coffee** and **cocoa**

Coffee beans give us coffee.

Tea leaves give us tea.

- **Sugar** from sugarcane.

Wood: We get wood from trees. It is used to make houses, furniture and many other items. It is also used as firewood.

Fibres: Plants give us fibres. Cotton fibres come from the cotton plant, jute fibre come from the jute plant and coir from coconut.

Medicines: We get medicines from plants such as neem, *tulsi*, turmeric, eucalyptus and poppy.

Neem

Tulsi

Turmeric

Some plants used as medicines

Perfumes: We get perfumes from flowers such as rose, jasmine and lavender.

Rubber: We get rubber from the rubber plant. It is used to make tyres and erasers.

Paper: We get paper mainly from the bamboo plant.

Rubber is made from the rubber tree

Paper is made from bamboo.

Learn more about photosynthesis; also see a video on photosynthesis.
http://photosynthesiseducation.com/photosynthesis-for-kids/

The recipe plants use to make food!
http://www.realtrees4kids.org/sixeight/letseat.htm

LINKED SITES

Keywords

Shoot	: Portion of the plant that grows above the ground.
Root	: Portion of the plant that grows below the soil.
Tap root	: A main thick root that grows from the end of the stem with several thinner roots emerging from it.
Fibrous root	: A number of equal-sized roots growing from the end of the stem.
Stomata	: Tiny openings present on the underside of the leaf blade.
Trunk	: Hard, woody and strong stem of a trees.
Photosynthesis	: Process by which plants make their food in the leaves.
Transpiration	: Release of water vapour from stomata in leaves

Points to Remember

◈ Roots fix the plant to the soil, and provide water and minerals to the plant.

◈ The stem supports the plant, and carries water and minerals to its leaves. It also carries food to all parts of the plant.

- Green leaves contain chlorophyll. They make food for the plant by photosynthesis.
- Plants use some of the food for getting energy, and for repair and growth.
- The extra food is turned into starch and stored in fruits, stems, leaves, roots or seeds.
- Leaves release extra water vapour from the plant through stomata. This is called transpiration.
- We get many different kinds of products from plants.

EXERCISE

1. **Fill in the blank boxes in the photosynthesis mind map.**

☐ From sunlight		Given off into air → ☐
☐ Absorbed by roots	→ LEAF →	
☐ Enters through stomata		☐ Part used up; rest stored

2. **Multiple Choice Questions (MCQs)**

   a. Which of these is a function of the root?
      (i) Fix the plant to the soil
      (ii) Absorb water
      (iii) Absorb minerals
      (iv) All of these

   b. In which of these plant parts is food made?
      (i) Fruit
      (ii) Stem
      (iii) Leaf
      (iv) Seed

   c. Which of these is *not* required for photosynthesis?
      (i) Sunlight
      (ii) Oxygen
      (iii) Water
      (iv) Carbon dioxide

   d. Energy needed by leaves to make food is obtained from:
      (i) Sunlight
      (ii) Food stored in plants
      (iii) Heat
      (iv) All of these

   e. The cabbage plant stores food in its:
      (i) Fruits
      (ii) Roots
      (iii) Leaves
      (iv) Stem

f. Plants use food for:

(i) Growth   (ii) Repair

(iii) Both (i) and (ii).   (iv) Neither (i) nor (ii)

3. **Match the columns.**

Column A	Column B
a. Stem	(i) Takes water and minerals from the soil
b. Root	(ii) Has seeds inside it
c. Leaf	(iii) Takes water up to the leaf
d. Fruit	(iv) Makes food

4. **Put ✓ for true, and ✗ for false.**

a. Potato is a root with food stored in it.

b. While making food, plants use up oxygen and give out carbon dioxide.

c. Plants make food at all times during day and night.

d. Plants do not need oxygen.

e. We get spices from plants.

5. **Name these.**

a. Type of root in grass.

b. Stem of a tree.

c. Very small openings in leaves.

d. Thin tubes spread over the leaf blade of a leaf.

e. The substance in leaves that absorbs the energy of sunlight.

f. Release of water vapour by a plant.

6. **What are the functions of the root?**

7. **How does the stem help a plant?**

8. **What are the things a plant needs to make food? How does it get each?**

9. **What does a plant use food for?**

10. **Give two ways in which transpiration is useful to a plant.**

11. **List three food items and three other products we get from plants.**

Thinking Questions

1. Plants give out water by transpiration and then draw more water through the roots. However, if plants do not give out water by transpiration they will not need to draw more water through the roots. This will save energy and will be good for plants. Do you agree? Give reasons.

2. What do you think will happen if there were no plants on the earth?

Science in everyday life

Besides providing food and other products, plants also clean the air by removing carbon dioxide and adding oxygen. You should plant trees and other plants around your house and look after them so that they grow well. They will make your house look beautiful and also make you healthier.

Fun to Do

Activity-1

Science experiment

1. Prepare a Leaf 'Skeleton'

- Take a few leaves that have fallen from the trees, and are dry.

- Take water in a pan and add about 2 tablespoonful of washing soda to it. Heat the pan until the water is nearly boiling.

- Stop heating the pan. Place the leaves in the pan and leave for about 30 minutes. Put the pan under a tap and let cold water flow for a few minutes.

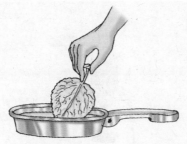

- You will find that the soft parts of the leaf fall off. The main vein and the side veins of the leaf can now be clearly seen. Dry and keep the leaf skeletons.

Note: Remember to do this experiment with an adult.

Activity-2

To test for starch in green leaves (Teacher demonstration)

You know that the food made in leaves is glucose, which is converted to starch. Therefore, starch should be present in a green leaf.

However, if a plant is kept in the dark for 24 hours, the leaves will not be able to make food. All the starch already present in the leaves will be used up. Then, the leaves of the plant will not show any starch.

Let us see if this is true. We can test for starch using iodine solution. When iodine solution is added to starch, it turns blue-black.

1. Take two similar potted plants. Place Plant 1 in the sun for a couple of hours. Place Plant 2 in a dark cupboard for 24 hours.

2. Pluck a leaf from Plant 1.

3. Keep the leaf in boiling water for a few minutes.

(a) Boil leaf in water

4. Place the leaf in a test tube containing alcohol (spirit). Heat the beaker in a larger beaker containing water (water bath). The leaf will lose chlorophyll and therefore its green colour.

(b) Boil in spirit in a water bath

5. Wash the leaf in water, keep it in a petridish and add a few drops of iodine solution to it.

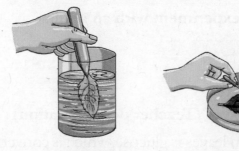

(c) Wash in water   **(d) Add iodine solution**

6. Does the leaf turn blue-black? This shows the presence of starch in the leaf.

7. Now pluck a leaf from Plant 2 and test it for starch in the same way. Does it show the presence of starch? You will find that it does not.

TEST PAPER–1

(Chapters 1 – 6)

A. Choose the correct answer(MCQs)

1. What is common between these animals – frog, newt, salamander?

    (a) They breathe only through lungs.

    (b) They breathe only through gills.

    (c) They breathe through lungs and gills.

    (d) They breathe through lungs and skin.

2. You get a toothache when a cavity in the tooth reaches the:

    (a) Crown   (b) Dentine

    (c) Pulp   (d) Gum

3. Which of these nutrients is very important but required only in very small quantities?

    (a) Proteins   (b) Carbohydrates

    (c) Minerals   (d) Fats

4. The lettuce plant stores food in its:

    (a) Fruits   (b) Roots

    (c) Leaves   (d) Stem

5. Where is the digested food absorbed into the blood?

    (a) Stomach   (b) Small intestine

    (c) Large intestine   (d) Mouth

B. Fill in the blanks.

1. Transpiration helps in ……………………..the plant.

2. The cactus plant stores water in its …………………..

3. The ……………….. helps to mix food with saliva.

4. …………………. is the portion of the tooth that has blood vessels.

5. The …………………………. system helps your body get rid of waste materials.

6. The camel has a hump on its back where ………….. is stored.

C. Answer the following questions.

1. Differentiate between energy-giving food and body-building food.

2. Why is excretion necessary?

3. With the help of labelled diagram explain the structure of a tooth.

4. Why do some trees lose their leaves in winter? What are such trees called?

5. What are the things a plant needs to make food? How does it get each?

6. List the adaptations found in aerial animals.

D. Label the following diagrams.

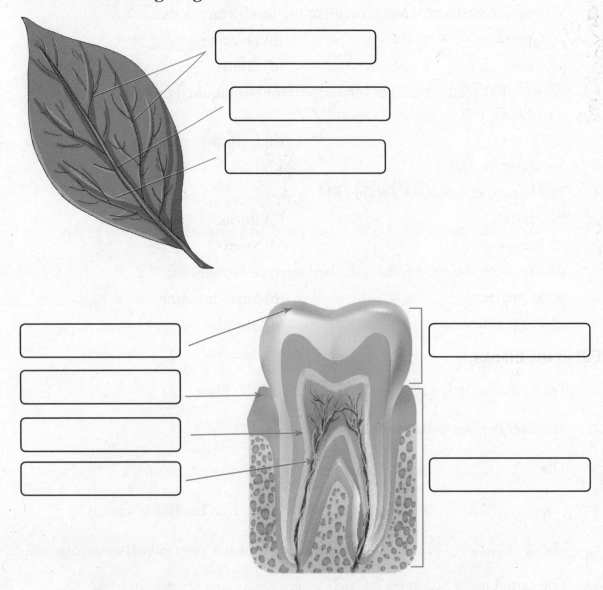

7

Air

Key Concepts

- Some properties of air i.e., occupy space, weight, expands, no colour.
- Composition of air (gases + water vapour).
- Process of breathing and burning.
- Causes of air pollution – dust, smoke, spitting (germs/bacteria, Virus), preventive measures to keep air clean.

Warming up

- Can you solve this riddle? What is all around you and is necessary for you to live but you cannot see it?

You cannot see air but it is all around you. Surrounding us is a thick blanket of air called the **atmosphere**. Without the atmosphere there would be no life on earth.

WHAT DOES AIR CONTAIN?

Air is a mixture of gases. It contains three main gases.

- More than three-fourths of air is a gas called **nitrogen**.
- About one-fifth is the gas **oxygen**.
- Small amount of some other gases including **carbon dioxide** are also present in air.

Besides these gases, air also contains **water vapour**, **dust** and **smoke**. The amount of these varies from place to place and from time to time.

HUMIDITY

Take a clean glass. Fill it half with water. Add some ice cubes to the water to make it cold. Observe the outside of the glass after some time. Can you see small drops of water on it? This water comes from air. Water vapour in the air changes back to water when it is cooled by the cold glass.

The amount of water vapour in air is called **humidity**. It varies according to the location of a place and the weather. A place near the sea, such as Chennai, has greater humidity than a place away from the sea such as Delhi. But Delhi also has high humidity during the monsoon season, when it rains a lot.

PROPERTIES OF AIR

Following are the properties of air.

Air has no colour

You cannot see the air around you because it has no colour.

Air does not have definite shape or volume

You have read in the previous class that air is a gas. Like all gases, *air does not have definite shape or volume.*

If you blow air into a balloon, it takes the shape of the balloon. If you now let the air out in a room, it will spread all over the room. It now takes up more space than it did inside the balloon.

Air Occupies Space

Hold up an empty glass. Is it really empty? Let us find out.

Crush a sheet of paper and press it into the bottom of the empty glass. Hold the glass upside down and insert it completely into a bowl of water without tilting it.

Crushed paper

Air

Water

Air occupies space

Take the glass out without tilting it. Feel the paper. Is it still dry? Why?

This activity shows that water was not able to enter the glass. This is because air occupied the space available in the glass.

Air Has Weight

Let us perform an activity to see if air has weight.

Take two footballs of the same size. Take out air from both the footballs. Place them on the two pans of a balance. If one of them is lighter than the other, put some sand on the pan with the lighter football to balance the pans.

Now fill one of the footballs tightly with air. Put it back on the pan. Is this football now heavier? It is heavier because of the weight of the air filled in it. This activity shows that air has weight.

Air has weight

USE OF AIR

Air is Needed for Burning

Fix a short candle on a plate and light it. Now invert a glass over the candle. You will find that the candle goes out in a few seconds.

The candle burnt for some time because there was air in the glass. Once the air is used up, the candle cannot continue burning.

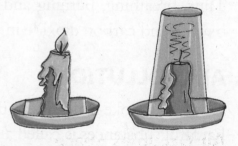

The part of air that is used up in burning is oxygen. Carbon dioxide is given out during burning.

Air is Needed for Breathing

Air is necessary for all living things for **breathing**. The air we breathe in is called **inhaled air**. The air we breathe out is called **exhaled air**. You know that our body uses the oxygen present in air and gives out carbon dioxide as waste. Therefore, exhaled air contains less oxygen and more carbon dioxide than inhaled air.

OXYGEN AND CARBON DIOXIDE IN AIR

You have seen that oxygen gets removed and carbon dioxide gets added to air during burning and breathing. This means that the amount of oxygen in the air should go on reducing and amount of carbon dioxide should go on increasing. But this does not happen. Why?

This is because, during the day, plants use up carbon dioxide and give out oxygen when they make food by the process of photosynthesis.

Thus, breathing, burning and photosynthesis together make sure that the amount of oxygen and carbon dioxide in the air remains the same.

AIR POLLUTION

Dust and smoke make the air dirty. The dirtying of air because of dust, smoke and other harmful substances is called air pollution.

Air Pollution

Causes of Air Pollution

The substances that cause air pollution are called **pollutants**. The main pollutants of air are:

- **Smoke** and **harmful gases** given off by vehicles, factories and burning fuels
- **Dust particles**
- **Germs:** Some germs are always present in air. Many more are added when people who are not well spit, cough or sneeze.

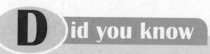

id you know

Electric vehicles produce less air pollutants.

Effects of Air Pollution on Our Body

When we breathe polluted air, harmful substances get into our body. Which body system do you think they will harm the most? The Respiratory System.

Why do you think the air during Diwali gets very heavily polluted? What can you do to prevent this?

Find out if anyone you know has a disease called **asthma**. Find out what happens when people with this disease breathe heavily polluted air, for example during Diwali.

Reducing Air Pollution

Some methods to control air pollution and keep the air clean are as follows.

- Plant more trees. Trees clean the air.
- Reuse and recycle waste materials and garbage instead of burning them.
- Use filters in vehicles and factories to prevent harmful gases from escaping into the air.
- Use bicycles and public transport instead of private vehicles, as much as possible. This will reduce pollution caused by vehicles.
- Save energy, including electricity – this will mean less fuels being burnt and reduced air pollution.
- Reduce waste - do not throw away food waste and plant waste such as leaves; instead, use them to make compost.
- People suffering from cold and cough should cover their mouths with a tissue or with their elbow when they cough or sneeze.

All about air pollution, including its history
http://www.clean-air-kids.org.uk/airquality.html

Learn to make a parachute
http://www.sciencekids.co.nz/experiments/freefall.html

Keywords

Atmosphere : Thick blanket of air around the earth.
Humidity : Amount of water vapour present in the air.
Air pollution : Dirtying of air because of dust, smoke and other harmful materials.

Points to Remember

◆ The main gases present in air are nitrogen, oxygen and carbon dioxide.
◆ The amount of water vapour in air is called humidity.
◆ Dust, smoke and germs pollute the air.
◆ Air occupies space, has weight, and is needed for burning and breathing.
◆ Oxygen is used and carbon dioxide is given out during breathing and burning.
◆ Plants use carbon dioxide and give out oxygen during photosynthesis.
◆ The dirtying of air because of dust, smoke and other harmful substances is called air pollution.
◆ Air pollution affects our respiratory system.
◆ We should take steps to reduce air pollution.

EXERCISE

1. **Fill in the blank boxes to show what air is made up of. The first letter of each is given.**

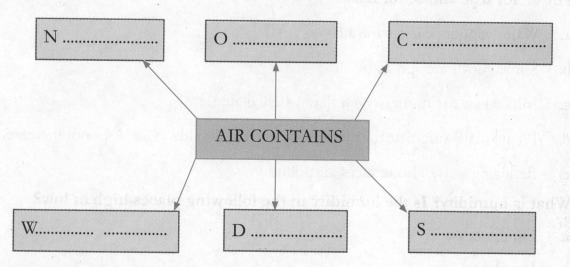

N ....   O ....   C ....

AIR CONTAINS

W............. ....   D ....   S ....

2. **Multiple Choice Questions (MCQs)**

   a. Which gas makes up most of air?

   (i) Oxygen   (ii) Carbon dioxide
   (iii) Nitrogen   (iv) Water vapour

b. The presence of which of these in air varies from place to place?

(i) Oxygen   (ii) Nitrogen

(iii) Carbon dioxide   (iv) Water vapour

c. Which of these is true for burning?

(i) Oxygen is formed

(ii) Carbon dioxide is formed.

(iii) Carbon dioxide is used up

(iv) Oxygen and carbon dioxide are neither formed nor used up

d. The amount of which of these gases in air is the least?

(i) Oxygen   (ii) Carbon dioxide

(iii) Nitrogen   (iv) None as all are present in equal quantities

e. Which of these is *not* true for air?

(i) It has no weight.   (ii) It occupies space.

(iii) It is needed for burning.   (iv) It is needed for breathing.

f. Which of these causes air pollution?

(i) Dust   (ii) Smoke

(iii) Germs   (iv) All of these

3. **Put ✓ for true and ✗ for false.**

a. Water vapour pollutes the air.

b. Some germs are spread by air.

c. Inhaled air has more oxygen than exhaled air.

d. Plants make sure that the amount of carbon dioxide in air does not increase.

e. Reducing waste also reduces air pollution.

4. **What is humidity? Is the humidity in the following places high or low?**

a. On the coast

b. In a desert

5. **You are suffering from common cold and cough. Why should you place a napkin or your elbow in front of your mouth when you cough or sneeze?**

6. **List two properties of air.**

7. **Which part of air is used up and which gas is given out during the following?**

   a. Burning

   b. Breathing

   c. Photosynthesis

8. **The amounts of carbon dioxide and oxygen in air do not change. Why?**

9. **List three ways by which pollution can be reduced.**

Thinking Questions

1. In which of the following cases will the candle burn for a longer time? Why?

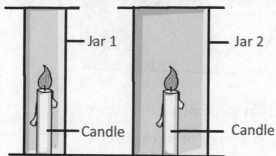

2. Suppose we cut down all trees on the earth. What effect will this have on the amounts of oxygen and carbon dioxide in the air?

Science in everyday life

Caring for the environment is the duty of each one of us. Reducing garbage is a way of showing that you care. Here are some ways of reducing garbage.

- Do not buy things that you do not need.
- Take a cloth bag with you when you go shopping, and do not take a plastic bag from the shopkeeper.
- If you have to take a plastic bag, use it several times and throw it away only when it tears.
- Buy goods that have less packaging. A product that is attractively packaged with a lot of packing material is more expensive because you are paying for the packaging as well. Also you create more garbage by buying such products.
- Reuse things as many times as possible. For example reuse bottles to store water

Think of more ways to reduce garbage.

Fun to Do

Activity

Make a model – a pinwheel

1. Take a square sheet of paper. Make cuts from its four edges up to about an inch from its centre.

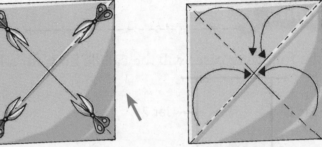

2. Fold as shown and paste the folded ends in the centre.

3. Pass a pin through the centre and fix it on a piece of stick.

4. Your pinwheel is ready. Rotate it a few times with your hand so that it turns freely about the pin.

5. Now take it to a place where the wind is blowing, or hold it in your hand and run.

   Does your pinwheel rotate in the wind?

8

Materials and Solutions

Key Concepts

- Definition- solvent, solute and solution, giving examples of each
- Soluble and insoluble substances giving examples of each (solubility in oil, water)
- Method of separation: sedimentation, decantation, filtration, evaporation.

Warming up

- When you open a bottle of a fizzy drink such as a cola, bubbles of a gas come out of the drink. Where do you think the bubbles come from? Are they water vapour bubbles or are they of some other gas?

SOLUTIONS

You read in Class 3 that if a little sugar is added to a glass of water and stirred, the sugar dissolves in water. We get a solution of sugar in water.

However, if some sand is added to a glass of water, the sand does not dissolve no matter how much you stir.

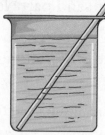

Sugar dissolves in water

Sand does not dissolve in water

Sugar is a **solute**. *The substance that dissolves in a liquid to form a solution is called a solute.* A solute can be a solid, liquid or gas.

Water is a **solvent**. *The liquid in which a solute dissolves is called a solvent.* Water is known as a universal solvent as it can dissolve many substances. Petrol is also a solvent.

Water and sugar form a **solution**. *A solution is the mixture formed when a solute dissolves in a solvent.* Some examples of solutions are:

- Seawater is a solution of salt in water.
- Fizzy drinks are a solution of a gas carbon dioxide in water. The bubbles that you see in a fizzy drink are of carbon dioxide.
- Fish breathe the gas oxygen dissolved in water.
- Oil dissolves in petrol to form a solution.

Fizzy drink

Sugar is **soluble** in water. *A substance that dissolves in a liquid is soluble in the liquid.* Some other substances that are soluble in water are salt, soap, dish washing liquid, orange juice and coffee.

Sand is **insoluble** in water. *A substance that does not dissolve in a liquid is insoluble in the liquid.* Mud, turmeric, chalk and oil are some other substances insoluble in water.

Take a little water in a glass. Add some cooking oil to it. Stir the mixture and then let it stand for some time. Do the water and oil separate out after some time? Which layer is on top – water or oil? This shows that oil is insoluble in water.

Oil in water

METHODS OF SEPARATION

Sometimes we have to separate soluble and insoluble substances from a solution. For example, we have to separate insoluble sand or mud from the water we use at home. Also, the salt we eat is made by separating it out from seawater.

Separating an Insoluble Solid from a Liquid

Sedimentation and decantation: Take some water in a beaker and mix a little sand in it. Do not disturb the mixture for a few minutes. Do the heavier sand particles settle down at the bottom of the beaker?

The sand that settles down is called **sediment**. The process of settling down of heavy insoluble particles in a liquid is called **sedimentation**.

After sedimentation has happened, carefully pour out the liquid on top by tilting the beaker. This is known as **decantation**.

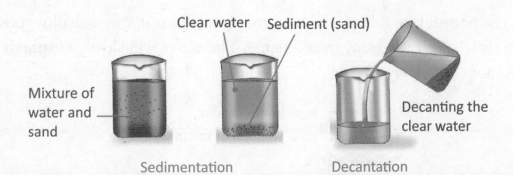

Clear water   Sediment (sand)

Mixture of
water and
sand

Decanting the
clear water

Sedimentation   Decantation

You can use sedimentation and decantation to separate heavy, insoluble particles from a liquid.

Filtration: You cannot separate a mixture of water and tea leaves by sedimentation and decantation. This is because many of the tea leaves will float on water. You can separate them by pouring the mixture through a sieve. A sieve has fine holes. Water can pass through the holes but tea leaves cannot. The tea leaves get left behind on the sieve.

Filtration

How will you separate a mixture of sand and water? Can you use the same sieve? Why not? The sand particles are very small and they can pass through the holes of the sieve. You need a sieve with very fine holes. You can use a **filter paper** for this. It has very fine holes.

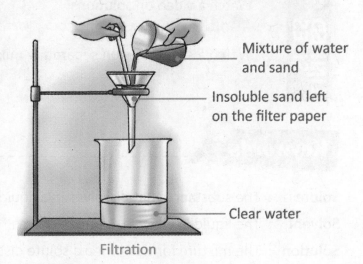

Mixture of water
and sand

Insoluble sand left
on the filter paper

Clear water

Filtration

Take a circular filter paper. Fold it twice and open it out to form a cone. Put it into a glass funnel. Put a beaker below the funnel. Pour the mixture of water and sand into the funnel, a little at a time. Clean water drip into the beaker. The sand is left on the filter paper.

This process is known as **filtration**.

Separating a Soluble Solid from a Liquid

You have a solution of salt in water. You want to get the salt back. How will you do this? You know that when you heat water, it evaporates. If you evaporate all the water in a solution of salt in water, you will get the salt back!

Dissolve a teaspoonful of salt in a little water. Pour the water in a shallow bowl (or an evaporating dish). Heat the bowl over a flame. The water will slowly evaporate. Let the water evaporate completely.

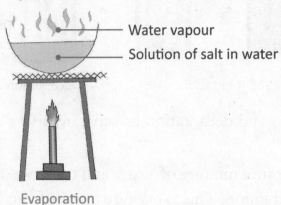

Water vapour

Solution of salt in water

Evaporation

Is there a white residue left behind in the dish? Scrape it out and taste it. Is it salty? You have got back the salt from a solution of salt in water by **evaporation**.

LINKED SITES

Watch a video on solutions
https://www.youtube.com/watch?v=e-2EoyDYamg

Watch a slide show on separating mixtures
http://slideplayer.com/slide/5669576/

Keywords

Solute : The substance that dissolves in a liquid to form a solution.

Solvent : The liquid in which a solute dissolves.

Solution : The mixture formed when a solute dissolves in a solvent.

Points to Remember

◈ A solution is formed when a solute (such as salt) dissolves in a solvent (such as water).

◈ Salt and sugar are soluble in water. Sand and mud are insoluble in water.

◈ An insoluble solid can be separated from a liquid by sedimentation and decantation, and by filtration.

◈ A soluble solid can be obtained from its solution by evaporation.

EXERCISE

1. **Multiple Choice Questions(MCQs)**

   a. Which of the following can dissolve in water?

   (i) Only solids   (ii) Only solids and liquids

   (iii) Solids, liquids and gases   (iv) Only liquids

   b. In a solution of sugar in water, sugar is:

   (i) Solvent   (ii) Solute

   (iii) Solution   (iv) Insoluble solid

   c. To separate a heavy, insoluble substance from water, you can use:

   (i) Sedimentation and decantation   (ii) Filtration

   (iii) Evaporation   (iv) Either (i) or (ii)

   d. Which of the following substances is insoluble in water?

   (i) Soap   (ii) Orange juice

   (iii) Coffee   (iv) Turmeric

   e. Dish washing liquid is................ in water.

   (i) Soluble   (ii) Insoluble

   (iii) Heavy   (iv) None of these

2. **Fill in the boxes.**

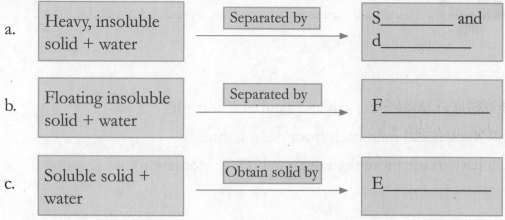

a. Heavy, insoluble solid + water → Separated by → S_____ and d_____

b. Floating insoluble solid + water → Separated by → F_____

c. Soluble solid + water → Obtain solid by → E_____

3. Put ✓ for true and ✗ for false.

   a. Water is the only solvent.

   b. Oil dissolves in water.

   c. Some gases can dissolve in water.

   d. A filter paper has very fine holes in it.

   e. Salt and water both evaporate on heating.

4. **What is a solution? Give three examples of solutions.**

5. **What is the difference between soluble and insoluble substances?**

6. **What happens when you mix water and cooking oil?**

7. **You have some water in a glass. You notice that very small pieces of wood are floating on the water. How can you separate them from the water?**

8. **How can you get back dissolved sugar from a solution of sugar in water?**

Thinking Questions

1. A bottle contains either salt or chalk. How will you find out what it has, without tasting it?

2. Suppose you are given a mixture of sand and fine particles of iron. How can you separate them? (Hint: you will have to use a method not given in the chapter. Think of something that can attract iron but not sand.)

Fun to Do

Activity

Take water in a beaker. Add some salt and sand in it and stir.

Now try to get the salt and sand back from the mixture.

(Hint: You will have to use more than one method of separation)

Light

Key Concepts

- Source of light: natural and artificial.
- Examples of sources of natural and artificial light.
- Luminous/non-luminous objects.
- Properties of light.
- Transparent, translucent and opaque objects. Examples of each category of objects.
- Uses of these objects in daily life.
- Formation of shadows (how a shadow is formed - not in technical terms).

Warming up

- Light : Think of as many things as you can which give out light. Arrange them into two groups - things that give bright light and things that give faint light.

LIGHT

Light is necessary for life. We are able to see things because of light. Plants use the energy of light to make food by photosynthesis. All living things depend on this food, either directly or indirectly.

Sources of Light

The sun gives us light. A glowing electric bulb and a burning candle also give us light. These are **sources of light**. Other sources of light are stars and glowworms. The sun is our main source of light.

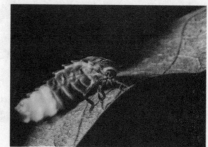

A glowworm

The sun, stars and glowworms are **natural** sources of light. The candle and the electric bulb are **artificial** sources of light. Artificial sources of light are made by humans.

Sources of light are also called **luminous objects**.

A table or a book does not give out its own light. We can see these objects when light falls on them. We cannot see them when it is dark. Objects that do not produce their own light are called **non-luminous objects**.

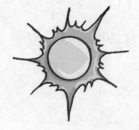

Natural source of light   Artificial source of light

How Light Travels

Have you seen a stream flowing? The path of water in the stream is not straight. It keeps changing its direction. If a large stone comes in its way, it bends around it. But light cannot bend in this way. It travels in straight lines.

Water keeps changing its direction

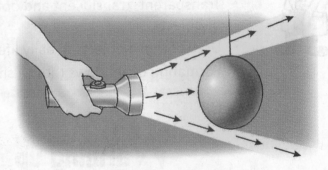

Light travels in straight lines

If you throw a ball towards a wall it bounces off. When light hits anything. it also bounces off. We call this **reflection** of light. If anything reflects light to our eyes, we can see that thing.

A ball bounces when it hits the wall

Reflection of light by a mirror and a book

SHADOWS

In a dark room, shine a flashlight towards a wall. Can you see the light from the torch on the wall?

Place your hand between the torch and the wall. Can you see the shadow of your hand on the wall?

Now switch off the flashlight. Can you see the shadow now?

The shadow of your hand is formed on the wall because your hand blocks the path of light from the flashlight to the wall.

When the path of light is blocked by anything, a **shadow** of that thing is formed. When you stand in the sun, you block the path of sunlight. This is why your shadow is formed.

Your shadow formed in sunlight looks like you. But sometimes it is smaller, and sometimes bigger than you. Can you say when it is smaller, and when it is bigger than you?

TRANSPARENT, TRANSLUCENT AND OPAQUE

Sunlight comes into your room through the glass windowpanes. You can also see through the windowpanes. This is because almost all light falling on the windowpane can pass through it.

Substances that allow almost all light to pass through them are called **transparent substances**. Other transparent substances are clear water and a thin plastic sheet.

Transparent glass window

Sunlight cannot come in through a wooden door. You can also not see through the wooden door. This is because wood does not allow any light to pass through it. Substances that do not allow any light to pass through them are called **opaque substances**. Metal, brick and thick plastic are also opaque.

Opaque wooden door

Look at the frosted glass windowpanes in your bathroom. Some light can come in through them. But can you see through them? No! Frosted glass and tracing paper allow some light to pass through them. But you cannot see clearly through them. Such substances are called **translucent substances**.

Translucent frosted glass window

Using Transparent, Translucent and Opaque Materials

We want sunlight to come in the rooms and kitchen of our house through the windows. We also want to see outside through them. Therefore, we use transparent glass in window panes in the rooms and kitchen. Spectacles are made of transparent glass or plastic so that you can see through them.

We want the light to enter into our bathrooms. However, we do not want anyone to see inside. Therefore, we use translucent frosted glass in the windowpanes in our bathrooms.

At night, we switch on the lights in our house. However, we do not want anyone outside to see inside our house. So we use curtains made of opaque material (cloth) to cover the window panes at night.

Activities with light and shadows:
http://sciencekids.co.nz/gamesactivities/lightshadows.html

Keywords

- -

Luminous objects : Objects that give out their own light.

Translucent substance : A substance that allows only some of the light to pass through it.

- ◈ Sun is a natural source of light. An electric bulb is an artificial source of light.
- ◈ Light travels in straight lines.
- ◈ A shadow is formed when the path of light is blocked.
- ◈ A transparent substance allows almost all light to pass through it.
- ◈ An opaque substance does not allow any light to pass through it.
- ◈ A translucent object allows some light to pass through it.

EXERCISE

1. **Fill in the boxes.**

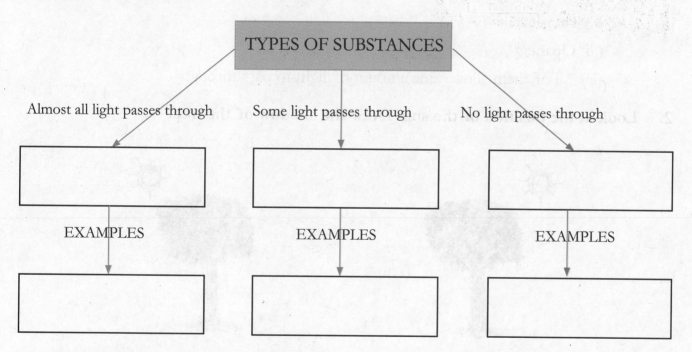

TYPES OF SUBSTANCES

| Almost all light passes through | Some light passes through | No light passes through |

EXAMPLES   EXAMPLES   EXAMPLES

2. **Multiple Choice Questions (MCQs)**

a. Which of these is *not* a source of light?

   (i) Candle   (ii) Electric bulb

   (iii) Moon   (iv) Sun

b. A shadow is formed when something:

   (i)   Reflects light   (ii) Blocks the path of light

   (iii) Produces light   (iv) Changes the path of light

c. Which of these is true for your shadow?

   (i)   It is always black.

   (ii) It is of the same colour as your clothes.

   (iii) It is always the same size as you.

   (iv) It is only formed when it is dark.

d. A ball is kept in front of the following. In which case is a shadow not formed?

   (i)   A lighted electric bulb   (ii) A lighted candle

   (iii) An electric torch that is switched off   (iv) Sunlight

e. Which of these kinds of substances allows the least amount of light to pass through?

   (i) Transparent

   (ii) Translucent

   (iii) Opaque

   (iv) All of them allow same amount of light to pass through

2. Look at the position of the sun. Draw the shadow of the tree.

a.

b.

4. Put ✓ for true and ✗ for false.

   a. Stars are sources of light

   b. You can see a ball only when it reflects light to your eyes.

   c. Light can go around anything blocking its path

   d. Shadows can be formed even when there is no light.

   e. Translucent substances do not allow any light to pass through them.

5. **Name these.**

   a. One source of light ....

   b. The bouncing off of light ....

   c. It is formed when light is blocked ....

   d. Light can pass through me but you cannot see clearly through me..........................

6. **What is the difference between luminous and non-luminous objects? Give two examples of each.**

7. **How is a shadow formed?**

8. **What is the difference between transparent and translucent objects? Give two examples of each.**

9. **Give two ways in which we use transparent substances.**

Thinking Questions

   1. Suppose light could bend around things blocking its path. Would shadows still be produced?

   2. Suppose a scientist discovered an object that does not give out its own light and also does not reflect any light. Would you be able to see such an object?

Science in everyday life

Very bright light can damage your eyes. Never look at the sun directly. Avoid looking directly at very strong sources of light, such as a searchlight.

Fun to Do

Activity

Science Experiments

1. Trace the front of a torch on a piece of cardboard.	2. Cut out the circle you have traced. Paste black paper on it.
3. Make a small hole in the centre using a sharp nail.	4. Tape this cardboard on the torch. Use black tape.

Perform experiments in a dark room to show the following.

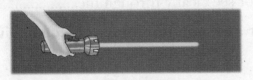 (a) Light travels in straight lines.	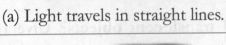 (b) Light is reflected by a mirror.
 (c) Light bends when it enters water.	(d) Light bends when it enters glass.

Measurements

Key Concepts

- Need for measurement
- Examples of measurement in daily life (buying goods, watching time)
- Simple description of instruments used for measurement (ruler, tape, weighing machine, thermometer, clock)
- Use of each instrument, how to read/use them.

Warming up

- Deepak asked his tailor to stitch a trouser for him. He told the tailor, 'the trouser should be 5 hand spans long'.
- The trouser was too long for Deepak!
- Can you say why?

NEED OF MEASUREMENT

The length of your hand span is different from that of an adult. So if everyone starts using their own hand spans to measure things there will be confusion! Just as in the case of Deepak's trouser!

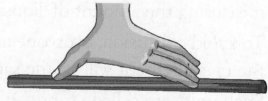

Hand span

MEASUREMENTS IN DAILY LIFE

We measure several things in our daily life, such as:

- The length of cloth required for a dress
- Your height and weight to see how much you have grown
- The weight of fruits and vegetables you buy
- The amount of petrol put in a car
- The time taken by you to reach school

Measuring Height   Weighing weight of vegetables   Filling Petrol

If measurements are not done properly, there will be confusion. For example you may buy too much or too little cloth for your dress. If you do not measure time properly you will reach school late.

STANDARD AND NON-STANDARD UNITS

Hand span is a **non-standard** unit of measuring length. Everyone has a different hand span.

You can use a mug to measure the amount of water that a bucket can hold. Mugs can be of different sizes. A mug is, therefore, a non-standard unit for measuring the amount of liquid.

To avoid confusion, everyone must use the same units of measurement. Then the measurement will be the same, no matter who measures it.

Such units are called **standard units**.

MEASURING LENGTH

To measure the length of a pencil or an eraser, we use a standard unit called a **centimetre**. It is written in short as **cm**. Your finger is about 1 cm thick.

Using a Ruler

You can use a **ruler** to measure length in centimetres. The ruler in your geometry box is 15 cm long. It can be used to measure things up to 15 cm. Longer rulers are 30 cm long.

To measure the length of a line, place the ruler along the line. One end of the line should be at the 0 cm mark. Read the length at the other end

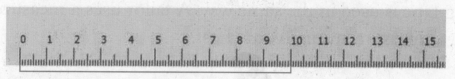

This line is 10cm long.

Using a metre scale and measuring tape

Longer distances such as the length of your room or the height of a tree are measured in a bigger unit called **metre**. It is written in short as **m**.

$$1\ m = 100\ cm$$

Spread your arms. The distance is about 1 metre.

A **metre scale** or a **measuring tape** can be used to measure length in metres.

Measuring tapes

A metre scale is 1 m long and is similar to a ruler. To measure with a metre scale, place it along the length being measured. One end of the length should be at the 0 cm mark of the metre scale. Read the length at the other end.

A measuring tape is used in the same way. A tailor uses a measuring tape that can be bent to measure around your chest.

Using a measuring tape to measure length of cloth

MEASURING WEIGHT

A paper clip

Measurement of weight tells us how heavy something is. The standard unit for measuring light things is the **gram** (**g**). A paper clip weighs about 1 gram.

To measure heavier things like the weight of fruits you buy or your own weight, the unit **kilogram** (**kg**) is used.

$$1 \text{ kg} = 1000 \text{ g}$$

Five medium size apples weigh about 1 kilogram.

You can use a **beam balance** or a **weighing machine** to weigh things.

To measure weight of apples with a weighing machine:

- Look at the needle of the machine without keeping anything on the pan. It should show 0 kg.

- Now place the apples on the pan.

- Take the reading of the needle. That gives the weight of the apples.

Weighing machine

To measure weight of apples with a beam balance:

- Look at the pans without keeping anything on the pan. They should be balanced.

- Now place the apples on the left pan and some weights on the right pan.

- Are the pans balanced?

- If not, change the weights on the left pan, pans will be balanced.

- The weights on the right pan now give the weight of the apples.

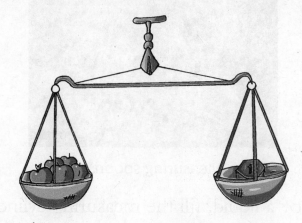

Beam balance

MEASURING VOLUME

The amount of liquid a container can hold is known as its **capacity**. A bucket can hold more liquid than a mug. Therefore the capacity of a bucket is higher.

The space occupied by a liquid is known as its **volume**. The capacity of a container is the same as the volume of liquid it can hold.

The standard unit for measuring capacity or volume is the **litre** (L). The capacity of a medium-sized mineral water bottle is 1 litre. It can hold 1 litre of water.

Smaller volumes are measured in the unit **millilitre** (mL).

$$1\,L = 1000\ mL$$

1 teaspoon contains about 5 mL medicine.

A glass can hold about 250 mL milk.

We use measuring cylinders, measuring beakers and measuring spoons to measure volume.

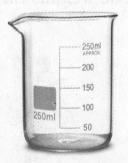

Measuring cylinder   Measuring spoons   Measuring beaker

If you want 200 mL of a liquid, fill the measuring cylinder or the measuring beaker up to the 200 mL mark with the liquid.

If you want 5 mL of medicine, use the 5 mL measuring spoon.

MEASURING TIME

A clock measures time. Time is measured in **hours** and **minutes**. You have learnt how to read a clock in your maths class. Can you say what time it is on these clocks?

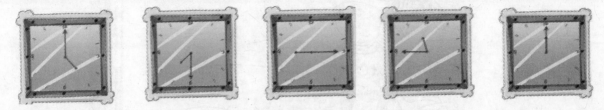

It is easier to read the time on a digital clock.

MEASUREMENT OF TEMPERATURE

Temperature tells us how hot or cold something is. We use a **thermometer** to measure temperature. We measure temperature in **degree Celsius**. It is written as °C.

It is the month of May in Delhi. The temperature is 40 degrees Celsius. Monu is feeling hot.

It is the month of December in Shimla. The temperature is 0 degrees Celsius. Rohan is feeling very cold.

Salman has a fever. His body temperature is 40 degree Celsius. His doctor says it should not be above 37 degree Celsius.

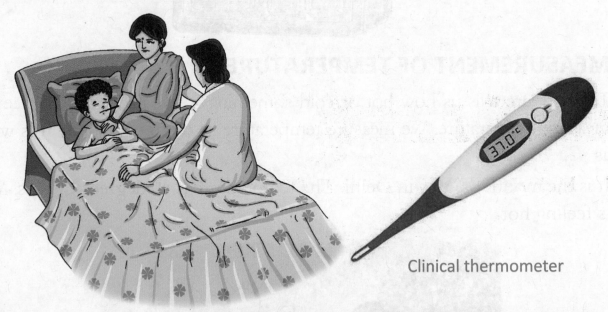

Clinical thermometer

108

Points to Remember

◈ It is important to use standard units when measuring anything.

◈ Some standard units are:

Length: metre, centimetre

Weight: Gram, kilogram

Capacity and volume: litre, millilitre

Time: hours, minutes

Temperature: degree Celsius

EXERCISE

1. **Multiple Choice Questions (MCQs)**

   a. You will measure the length of a pencil by using a:

   (i) Weighing scale   (ii) Ruler

   (iii) Hand span   (iv) Thermometer

   b. You will measure the height of a door by using a:

   (i) Weighing scale   (ii) Ruler

   (iii) Hand span   (iv) Measuring tape

   c. Who has fever?

   (i) Anil, 37°C   (ii) Binto, 36°C

   (iii) Nafisa, 40°C   (iv) Both Binto and Nafisa

d. You will measure 100 mL of water by using a:

   (i) Measuring cylinder   (ii) Measuring beaker

   (iii) Measuring spoon   (iv) Either (i) or (ii)

2. Put a ✓ on the best unit for measuring the following:

a. Length of a mobile phone: cm/m/g

b. Height of your house: cm/m/kg

c. Weight of a television: g/kg/m

d. Volume of soup in a bowl: mL/L/g

e. Distance travelled by a car in 1 hour: m/km/L

f. Volume of water in a bucket: mL/L/m

g. Weight of a coin: g/kg/cm

3. Fill in the blanks.

a. We must use .... units to measure things otherwise there will be confusion.

b. 1 m = ...cm

c. 1 kg = ...g

d. 1 L = ... mL

4. **Name a standard unit to be used in the following situations.**

   a. Buying vegetables ....

   b. Buying petrol for a car ....

   c. Buying cloth to stitch clothes ....

5. **Match the temperatures.**

Column A		Column B
a.	45°C	(i) Hot
b.	1°C	(ii) Pleasant
c.	10°C	(iii) Very hot
d.	25°C	(iv) Very cold
e.	35°C	(v) Cold

6. **Write the names of the instruments.**

   _____   _____

Thinking Questions

1. Five children of Class 4A measured the length of their classroom. They got different results. What could be the reason?

2. You are going to a hill station for a holiday. You are told that the temperature there during the day is 10°C.

   a. What kind of clothes will you pack for the trip?

   b. What do you think the night temperature will be?

Project

Measure you height

Stand against a wall. Ask a friend to hold a ruler horizontally on your head. Let him put a mark on the wall where the ruler touches the wall. Now measure the height from the bottom of the wall to the mark in centimetres, using a measuring tape. This is your height.

Measure the heights of 5 of your friends in the same manner way. Arrange them in increasing order of heights.

Activity

Find the capacity of a bucket

You will need a measuring cup for this. The cup has volume markings on its side.

Fill the cup up to the 500 mL mark. Empty it in the bucket. Do this until the bucket is full. How many times did you fill the cup?

Multiply by 500 mL to get the capacity of the bucket. Convert to litres by dividing the answer by 1000.

11 Push and Pull

Key Concepts

- The concept/ meaning of push and pull and difference between the two;
- Examples of push and pull.
- Force: meaning in simple terms, changes shape of objects and direction;
- Meaning of various types of forces – muscular, gravitational, magnetic and frictional.

Warming up

- To move a football, you can lift it in your hands. In what other ways can you move it?

PUSHES AND PULLS

When you have to move something, what do you do?

You either push it or pull it.

When you kick a football, you push it.

When you lift a football with your hands, you pull it towards yourself.

How many times do you push or pull something every day?

- You pull a drawer to open it. You push to close it.
- You push a cricket ball with your bat.
- You pull a book towards yourself, if you want to pick it up.

What other pushes and pulls can you see in the picture?

A push or a pull is called a **force**. A force can do many things.

- It can make an object **move**.

- It can **slow down** or **stop** a moving object.

- It can **change the direction** of moving objects.

- It can also **change the shape** of an object.

Types of Forces

There are many different types of forces. Let us study some that we come across often in our daily life.

Muscular Force

When you push or pull something, you apply force by using parts of your body such as feet or legs. You use the power of the muscles of your body. Such a force is called **muscular** force. All the forces you have seen above are muscular forces.

Gravitational Force or Gravity

Throw up a ball. Observe it carefully. It slows down, stops, and then comes down. Why doesn't it keep going up? This is because of **gravitational force** or **gravity** pulls everything down. You are able to stand on the ground because gravity pulls you down. If there was no gravity we would all be floating in air!

Friction

Roll a ball on the ground. Does it slow down and stop? Why does it not keep going?

Ball rolled on rough surface   Ball rolled on smooth surface

It stops because a force called **friction** acts on it. The ball will go further on a smooth surface than on a rough surface. This is because the force of friction is more on rough surfaces. It is less on smooth surfaces.

Magnetic Force

Bring a magnet close to iron nails. Do the nails get attracted to the magnet?

Now try with a steel spoon, a steel pin, an aluminium spoon, a plastic spoon, and a piece of paper. Do these get attracted to the magnet? Fill in the table.

Object	Pulled by a magnet?
Iron nail	Yes
Steel spoon	
Steel pin	
Aluminium spoon	
Plastic spoon	
Piece of paper	

A magnet applies a force on things made of iron and steel. It pulls things made of iron and steel towards itself. This force is called **magnetic force**.

The magnet does not pull things made of other substances such as paper, plastic and aluminium.

LINKED SITES

Learn more about energy sources—click on the source you want to know about..
http://www.kidzworld.com/site/p1423.htm

Interesting energy facts.
http://www.sciencekids.co.nz/sciencefacts/energy.html

Keywords

Force : An act of push or pull.

Magnetic force : Force that pulls things made of iron and steel towards itself.

Points to Remember

◈ Push or a pull is called a force.

◈ Force can move an object, stop a moving object, change the direction of a moving object, or change the shape of an object.

◈ There are many types of forces, for example muscular force, gravitational force, friction and magnetic force

1. **Fill in the blank boxes with names of five types of forces.**

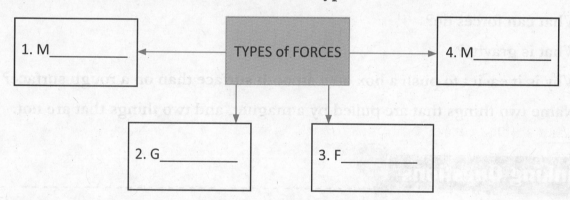

2. **Multiple Choice Questions (MCQs)**

   a. In which of these is a force *not* being applied?

      (i) Reading a book   (ii) Trying to push a wall

      (iii) Kicking a football   (iv) Throwing up a ball

   b. Which of these is a pull?

      (i) Kicking   (ii) Lifting

      (iii) Hitting   (iv) All of these

c. An apple falls from a tree. It falls down instead of going up because of:
   (i) Gravity   (ii) Friction
   (iii) Muscular force   (iv) Magnetic force
d. Which of these will be attracted to a magnet?
   (i) A steel clip   (ii) A plastic toy
   (iii) An iron hammer   (iv) Both (i) and (iii)

3. **Fill in the blanks.**
   a. A push or pull is a _____.

   b. If there was no _____ force we would all be floating in air.

   c. A rough surface has greater _____ than a smooth surface.

   d. _____ force can pull things made only of iron and steel.

4. **Put ✓ for true and ✗ for false.**
   a. Gravity pulls everything down.
   b. A force can change the weight of an object.
   c. A magnet pulls everything towards itself.
   d. Muscular force can only push and not pull.

5. **What can forces do?**
6. **What is gravity?**
7. **Why is it easier to push a box on a smooth surface than on a rough surface?**
8. **Name two things that are pulled by a magnet, and two things that are not.**

Thinking Questions

1. When astronauts go into outer space they float around in their spaceship. Which force is missing in outer space?

Fun to Do

Activity-1

Scientific investigation

Wind exerts a force

When the wind is blowing very hard try running (or cycling):

- against the wind

- in the direction of the wind

In which case does it take more effort to run (cycle)? Why?

Blowing wind exerts a force. If you run against the wind direction this force slows you down. If you run in the direction of the wind, it helps you to move faster.

Now you can understand why trees often get uprooted in a storm.

Friction as a Force

Key Concepts

- Friction – meaning, concept.
- How to reduce friction (oil, powder).
- Uses of friction.
- Harmful effects of friction.
- Examples of friction.

Warming up

- Suppose you roll a ball on a surface that does not have any friction at all. What do you think will happen to the ball?

FRICTION AND MOVING OBJECTS

In the previous chapter you read about the force of friction. You saw that it is a force that tries to stop an object moving on a surface.

A smooth surface has less friction than a rough surface. That is why a moving ball goes further on a smooth surface that on a rough surface. If a ball is rolled on a surface with no friction, it would go on moving without stopping!

Making an Object Move

Look at the pictures. Two heavy boxes have to be moved by pushing them. Anil is pushing the box kept on a smooth surface. Nirmala is pushing the box kept on a rough surface.

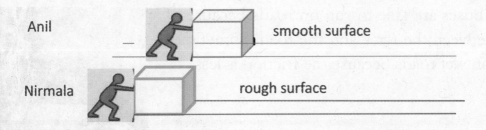

Anil — smooth surface

Nirmala — rough surface

Who will find it easier to move the box? Anil or Nirmala? Why?

If the box is kept on a smooth surface, less force is required to move it.

If the box is kept on a rough surface, greater force is required to move it.

This is because of friction.

So we now know that:

- A moving object will go further if the friction is less.
- A stationary object will be easier to move if the friction is less.

Friction – Good or Bad?

- Friction wastes energy because it makes it difficult for things to move. A machine such as a car works better if the friction between moving parts is less.
- The soles of your shoes wear away after some time because of fiction with the road surface.
- Friction causes moving machine parts to wear out. So the parts have to be changed after some time.

But friction is not always bad.

- You are able to walk because of friction between your feet and the ground. Without friction you will slip and fall. Have you ever tried to walk on ice? Why is it difficult? Ice is very smooth, and so there is very little friction and you can slip easily.
- You can ski on snow because there is very little friction between the ski and snow.

- Cars and buses are able to run on roads because of friction between the tyres and the road. Sometimes, cars slip on wet roads because the friction is less.

Reducing Friction

Take a carom board. Place the striker on it and hit it with your fingers. See how far it goes before coming to a stop.
Now spread talcum powder all over the board. Again hit the striker with the same force. See how far it goes now. Does it go further? Why?

Talcum powder is smooth. It reduces the friction on the board. So the striker travels further.

Making surfaces that rub against each other smooth by polishing and smoothening them, reduces friction between them.

Oiling reduces friction between surfaces because it makes the surfaces smooth. If you put oil on the moving parts of your bicycle, it will run more smoothly.

LINKED SITES

More on friction
http://www.bbc.co.uk/bitesize/ks2/science/physical_processes/friction/read/1/

Keywords

Friction : A force that tries to stop an object moving on a surface.

Points to Remember

◈ Friction is a force that tries to stop an object moving on a surface.

◈ Friction makes it difficult to move a stationary object on a surface.

◈ Friction is sometimes good and sometimes bad.

◈ Friction can be reduced by making the surfaces smooth, by polishing or oiling.

EXERCISE

1. Multiple Choice Questions (MCQs)

a. Which of these is *not* possible without friction?

   (i) Walking   (ii) Cars running on roads

   (iii) Jumping up   (iv) Both (i) and (ii)

b. The bad thing about friction is that it:

   (i) Wastes energy   (ii) Causes wear and tear

   (iii) Saves us from slipping   (iv) Both (i) and (ii)

c. Walking on slippery ground is difficult because there is:

   (i) Very little gravity between you and the ground

   (ii) Very high gravity between you and the ground

   (iii) Very little friction between your feet and the ground

   (iv) Very high friction between your feet and the ground

d. Which of these reduces friction?

   (i) Making surfaces smooth

   (ii) Putting oil between surfaces

   (ii) Putting smooth powder between surfaces

   (iv) All of these

2. What is friction?

3. Why can you slide easily on ice but not on your house floor?

4. List two problems that friction causes.

5. List two ways in which friction is useful to us.

6. How can you reduce friction between two surfaces?

Science in everyday life

Be very careful if you have to walk on a smooth tiled floor on which someone has spilled water. You can easily slip on it since friction on such a surface is low.

Check your car or scooter tyres. Have they got worn out? If so they must be changed. Otherwise the car or scooter can slip on a wet road.

Thinking Questions

1. Would you like to live in a world without friction? Give reasons.

Fun to Do

Activity-1

Scientific investigation

Test for Friction

1. Take a piece of plane wood. Use books to keep it in an inclined position on a table, as shown. Keep a block of wood below it.

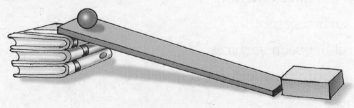

2. Roll a cricket ball on the inclined wood. It hits the wooden block and makes it move. Note the distance moved by the block.

Now keep a piece of smooth paper below the block. Use tape to fix it to the table. Again roll the ball. Does the block move more now? Which surface has greater friction? The table or the smooth paper?

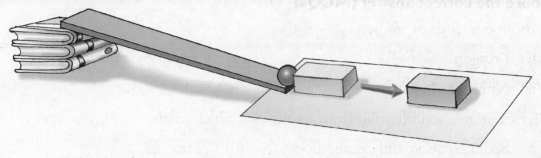

3. Try the experiment on other surfaces such as sandpaper or a table with sunmica fixed on it.

TEST PAPER–2

(Chapters 7 – 12)

A. Choose the correct answer (MCQs)

1. About one-fifth of air is:

   (i) Oxygen

   (ii) Carbon dioxide

   (iii) Nitrogen

   (iv) Water vapour

2. To separate a soluble solid from a solution, which method will you use?

   (i) Sedimentation and decantation

   (ii) Filtration

   (iii) Evaporation

   (iv) Either (i) or (ii).

3. Which of these kinds of substances allows the most light to pass through it?

   (i) Transparent

   (ii) Translucent

   (iii) Opaque

   (iv) None of them allow light to pass through them

4. Which of these will be attracted by a magnet?

   (i) A steel spoon

   (ii) A wooden spoon

   (iii) A plastic spoon

   (iv) A cardboard spoon

5. Which of these will increase friction?

   (i) Oiling the surfaces

   (ii) Making surfaces rough

   (iii) Putting powder between the surfaces

   (iv) Making surfaces smooth

B. Fill in the blanks.

1. Soles of shoes wear out because of _____ between the soles and the ground.

2. The force of _____ pulls everything down.

3. _____ is measured in degree Celsius.

4. When something blocks the path of light a _____ is formed.

5. Sugar dissolves in water to form a _____.

6. Smoke and harmful gases _____ the air.

C. Answer the following questions.

1. List three properties of air.

2. How will you make a solution of sugar and water? Name the solvent and solute in the solution.

3. What do you mean by a 'source' of light? Name two sources of light and two things which are not sources of light.

4. Why do we use standard units for measurements?

5. What is a force? Give three examples of forces.

6. You can walk easily on a tiled floor. But you can slip if the floor has some water on it. What effect does water have on the floor?

D. Look at the illustration and answer the questions.

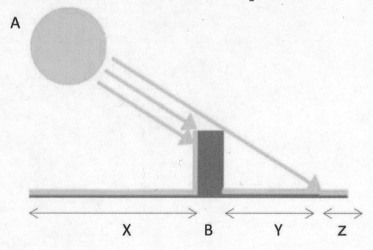

1. The object A gives out its own light. It is a _____ of light.

2. The object B stops all light from passing through it. It is a _____ object.

3. Which portion does not receive any light – X, Y or Z?

4. What is formed in the portion that does not receive any light?

E. The pie chart shows what air is made up of.

1. Which gas does the blue portion represent – carbon dioxide, oxygen or nitrogen?

2. Which gas does the red portion represent – carbon dioxide, oxygen or nitrogen?

3. The yellow portion represents other gases. Which is the most important of these 'other gases'?